CAN YOU BELIEVE IN GOD AND EVOLUTION?

CAN YOU BELIEVE IN GOD AND EVOLUTION?

A GUIDE FOR THE PERPLEXED

TED PETERS
MARTINEZ HEWLETT

ABINGDON PRESS
Nashville

CAN YOU BELIEVE IN GOD AND EVOLUTION?
A GUIDE FOR THE PERPLEXED

Copyright © 2006 by Abingdon Press

This book is printed on acid-free paper.

Library of Congress Cataloging-in-Publication Data

Peters, Ted, 1941-
   Can you believe in God and evolution? : a guide for the perplexed / Ted Peter and Martinez Hewlett.
      p. cm.
   Includes bibliographical references.
   ISBN 0-687-33551-5 (pbk. : alk. paper)
   1. Evolution—Religious aspects—Christianity. 2. Evolution (Biology)—Religious aspects—Christianity. 3. Creationism. 4. Bible and evolution. 5. Religion and science. I. Hewlett, Martinez J. (Martinez Joseph), 1942- II. Title.

   BL263.P46 2006
   231.7'652—dc22

                                                                            2006003169

ISBN 13: 978-0-687-33551-0

All scripture unless otherwise noted is from the King James or Authorized Version of the Bible.

Scripture noted NRSV is from the *New Revised Standard Version of the Bible*, copyright 1989, Division of Christian Education of the National Council of the Churches of Christ in the United States of America. Used by permission. All rights reserved.

Glossary is from *Evolution from Creation to New Creation* by Peters and Hewlett © 2003 Abingdon Press. Used by permission.

Graphic on page 55 is from *Evolution from Creation to New Creation* by Peters and Hewlett © 2003 Abingdon Press. Used by permission.

Text from "Evolutionary Psychology: A Primer" on page 33 is copyright 1997 by Leda Cosmides and John Tooby. Used by permission.

07 08 09 10 11 12 13 14 15—10 9 8 7 6 5 4 3 2

MANUFACTURED IN THE UNITED STATES OF AMERICA

CONTENTS

PREFACE

We are seriously concerned about two aspects of the culture war over evolution. First, confusion abounds. Nearly everyone is perplexed. We wrote our first book, *Evolution from Creation to New Creation*, to help clarify the confusion. Second, we are concerned about what the war over evolution might be doing to our young people in our schools and in our churches. Our fear is that they might begin to identify their Christian faith with anti-Darwinism and, worse, antiscience. This would be a tragedy. By no means do we want to baptize the Darwinian model of evolution, to be sure. Science does not absolutize its models, nor should we. Yet, we want our young people to fill the ranks of tomorrow's scientists. We believe both our schools and churches should encourage the idea that science can become a divine vocation.

This is our second book on this topic, intended to complement the first. As the culture war heats up over the impact of Charles Darwin's evolutionary theory on our schools and on our society's state of mind, the present book offers a couple of ways to arm you, the reader, for battle in what the cover of *Time* magazine for August 15, 2005, calls the "Evolution Wars." We offer understanding. We are now on a battlefield. While we may not have chosen to be here, we cannot avoid the battle. And, there is such a cloud of confusion. Warriors in our churches, in our schools, and in our courts are firing at us—and at each other—with no clear understanding of who should be in their sights or why. In this brief book, we will attempt to identify just who the warriors are, why they are fighting, and against whom. Once we clear away some confusing smoke, one item should become visible, namely, that no war is being fought between science and religion. Certainly no war is being fought between the Christian faith and research science. To persist in this confusion may lead to firing at one's friends rather than any true enemies that might be out there.

Another way to prepare for battle is to defend what is most valuable: our belief that the best science and our best thinking about God belong together. In this book we offer a way to integrate science with faith. This involves a confident Christian faith that can tolerate, if not embrace, the best science. The best science of today is the Darwinian or neo-Darwinian model for understanding biological change. In this book we will offer an integrated picture where the work of God incorporates evolution within an inclusive vision of divine creation and redemption.

Faith seeks understanding, said St. Anselm. Faith aiming toward expanded understanding is the path we will follow here. This is a path we hope will lead to a comprehensive picture of a magnificent creation with God the Creator and all creatures as beloved.

This book may introduce you to a number of new words and concepts. Do not be timid. We will guide you as we travel together. There is also a glossary at the end of the book. As the book winds its way along the trail of Darwinian and neo-Darwinian science, past the forests of creationism and Intelligent Design, past the raging rivers of controversy, into the meadow of theistic evolution, and upward toward fuller understanding, you the reader will hear us singing or humming at least five tunes.

First, we sing hymns of thanksgiving for the Bible's promise of resurrection and the advent of a transformed creation. We take seriously the prophetic vision of Isaiah 11 where the lion will lie down with the lamb and where all of nature will be at peace. It is here in the promise of new creation that we find God's purpose for the present created order. We believe in God's intention to draw all things in creation to their consummate fulfillment. In the promise of a new creation, we find God's purpose for us and all creation now.

This means, among other things, we do not easily find God's purpose in some sort of inner design or guide secretly operating within biology. Because the new creation will require something definitively new, we do not expect the old to provide what the new requires. Only God's promise can provide that. If we are to see purpose within natural processes, we will need to look through the lenses of God's promise for a transformed natural order. Only the eyes of the faith can see this. It will be invisible to a scientist looking through a microscope or telescope. This is not a criticism of science. It is only a recognition of the relationship between science and faith.

Second, we whistle occasionally about the difference between the way God acts and the world acts. We make a distinction, as did that great medieval theologian St. Thomas Aquinas, between thinking of God as primary creator of all things, and thinking of God as giving creation the freedom or openness to participate in influencing its own development. We believe God does more than create in some distant past; God invites us to step into a future that creation itself can help shape. As we look back into history we can see a record of these steps taken by nature and humanity. And we can look and learn from nature's history. The parts of history that science explores are the new forms of biological self-organization. God is the primary or first cause. Secondary causation results from the interaction and relationships of creatures to each other and to the created world.

Third, we sing a refrain: "God provides a purpose *for* nature but not *within* nature." God's purpose for nature, we believe, can be understood in analogy to human purpose. We know from experience that we use various objects in our environment for specific purposes. We will even refashion or redesign them to meet these purposes. We will cut a tree, saw the lumber, and build a chair—all for the purpose of sitting. The chair did not exist already in the tree. The tree became a chair due to the design of the person with a purpose. Similarly, we do not expect scientists to discern God's purpose or design within natural processes themselves. Scientists can marvel at the emergence of new and complex systems of life, such as a beautiful tree, to be sure; but we do not expect scientists to appeal to primary rather than secondary causation when analyzing them.

Fourth, we ask: how can we sing a song that harmonizes dissonant chords such as God's love for the world with suffering, death, sin, and evil? How could a God of love design a world of dog-eat-dog or survival of the fittest? How can we ascribe to God's will the necessity of life to get nourishment from the predator-prey relationship and the extinction of 90 percent of all species? Alfred Lord Tennyson's nature, "red in tooth and claw," does not fit easily with what we read in Genesis 1:1–2:4a, where God declares the creation to be "very good." This conflict cannot be resolved by saying that an intervening God is responsible for the design of nature's complex life forms.

We start to write this music by listening first to the New Testament, to what is revealed about God in the death and resurrection of Jesus. Here we find that God is gracious. God is loving to the poor, the marginalized, the sick, the crippled, the helpless, the sinners. God is also powerful, offering salvation through transformation, especially resurrection from the dead. So we ask: could we apply what we learn from Jesus Christ to our understanding of God's relationship to the natural world? We cautiously say yes. We then appeal to the Bible with its accompanying promise of resurrection and new creation.

Fifth, and finally, we chant: "public and religious schools should teach the best science." We owe our children the best we can give. Because, as St. Anselm said, faith seeks understanding, we believe the Christian faith is inherently interested in pursuing the best science. We Christians would not want anything less from our churches or schools. At our point in history, the Darwinian model (inclusive of the neo-Darwinian synthesis of evolution and genetics) provides the best science. We say this because the Darwinian model continues to yield new, useable knowledge not only about our planet's past but also about today's biology. It leads to the development of new and desperately needed medical therapies. Darwinism is good for our health, so to speak. Families of young people in our schools should demand that only the best science be provided for their education. And pastors in our congregations should offer wise counsel and encourage families and schools to make this demand.

But what about other approaches to evolution such as scientific creationism or Intelligent Design? These simply cannot offer what we need to better our world, even though they certainly want to. Both creationists and Intelligent Design (ID) supporters want a better world; they want the benefits of science. Everyone in the battle celebrates good science. In addition, creationists and ID supporters would like science to provide confirmation for their religious faith. In sum, they have a high regard for good science. So do we.

Yet, we find a problem here. Scientific creationists and Intelligent Design supporters may be deluding themselves when they seek to provide a better science than Darwinism. They believe that their own view of evolution constitutes superior science. However, we believe what they offer fails to meet the criterion of good healthy science. In fact, we do not believe it is science at all.

What they offer fails because it is not fertile and is not falsifiable. It does not lead to a progressive research program that will eventually blossom into new and expanded understanding of the natural world and, at the same time, yield its place before the weight of contradictory evidence. The criteria of fertility and falsifiability are much more important in determining good science than truth. The value of science is that it leads to ongoing research and new knowledge. Regardless of their truth value, the original Darwinian and neo-Darwinian models of evolution meet the criteria of fertility and falsifiability.

Even if promoted by conscientious and well-meaning Christian people, neither scientific creationism nor Intelligent Design constitute science in a way that gives us benefits equal to what the Darwinian model can give. Nevertheless, we applaud a contribution made by both scientific creationists and Intelligent Design supporters. It is their willingness to combat ideologies such as social Darwinism and materialistic atheism. These ideologies are, in fact, enemies of both the Christian value of compassionate love and the Christian affirmation of the existence of a gracious God. Religious critics of our public school system are right when they ask that our children be protected from overt atheism taught with public endorsement.

What makes our present situation difficult is this: the good science frequently comes shrink-wrapped in nonscientific ideologies such as atheistic materialism or even social Darwinism. We all know how exasperating it is to buy an item from the supermarket and then struggle to get the package open. The shrink-wrapping looks at first like it is part of the product. Only after poking and jabbing with sharp instruments do we finally liberate the nourishing food from the wrapping. Similarly, liberating the fertile science of the Darwinian model of evolution requires separating it from the ideologies in which it frequently comes packaged.

We understand the frustration and anger many Christian families have over the apparent endorsement of evolutionary biology and marginalizing of religious values in our public schools. Yet, we do not want the valuable product thrown out with the confounded wrapping. We insist that research science and the teaching of the best science be identified, then protected and fostered and enhanced. We cannot allow the quality of our science to be compromised while battling against ideology.

Now, you might ask, who are the authors of this book? There are two of us. One is a molecular biologist, a university and medical school professor who teaches the Darwinian and neo-Darwinian models of evolution. When Marty goes into the classroom or laboratory, he must be armed with the most fruitful scientific theory available. The Darwinian tradition provides this. In good conscience, he cannot offer anything inferior. Nearly daily he studies the recognized journals in his field; and over the years he has performed numerous experiments to test hypotheses. He is the coauthor of a frequently revised and widely read textbook in virology. Marty Hewlett embodies science in its progressive and fertile form. And because his research contributes to the development of medical therapies, his work indirectly has life-and-death implications. He needs to get it right. Nothing less than providing the best science could possibly give adequate expression to his earnest desire to serve God and serve the welfare of humanity.

The other coauthor is a systematic theologian. Ted teaches Christian theology to seminarians preparing to become pastors and to doctoral students preparing to become professors. Among the various tasks of today's theologian, he sees a need to construct a worldview in which all-important things are oriented toward the God of grace. This worldview necessarily includes natural science. The theologian needs to develop a healthy view of the relationship between faith and science, and parish pastors need to be prepared to provide healthy guidance to their congregations in this area. Ted Peters believes that the gospel is central to the Christian faith, and to tell the gospel is to tell the story of Jesus Christ with its significance. The story of Jesus Christ has significance for how we understand not just human nature, but also all of the natural world as well.

Marty is a Roman Catholic. Ted is a Lutheran. We are both intellectually curious; and we both care deeply about serving God's mission for all God's beloved creatures in this beautiful world.

We have been working together on our study of evolution for a half decade at this writing. We summarized our research in a more comprehensive book, *Evolution from*

Creation to New Creation (Abingdon 2003). What we offer now in this smaller book is an abridgement and update of the earlier work with an added emphasis on what pastors, congregations, schoolteachers, parents, and young adults might want to think about this important and intellectually exciting subject. Thus, we commend this book to you, the reader, that your faith finds a deeper and richer understanding, and that we, together, will blaze a peaceful path through the public battlefield.

Ted Peters
Martinez Hewlett
Epiphany, January 6, 2006

CHAPTER ONE

IS THERE A BATTLE IN OUR CLASSROOMS AND CONGREGATIONS?

As we already mentioned, one of us is a pastor and theologian while the other is a scientist and philosopher. Marty has taught biology at all levels of the university, from graduate and medical school to beginning courses, for over 30 years, primarily at the University of Arizona. He has seen firsthand the results of the battle in the lives of students, what some think of as a conflict between science and faith. The following is Marty's firsthand account of what happened in the case of two students whose stories typify the crisis. It is a crisis for both classroom and congregation.

Marty's Two University Students Caught in the Crossfire

This is the story of two of my students in Intro Biology. The first one—I'll call him Robert—took my beginning course with aspirations of becoming a wildlife biologist. He was an outstanding student, always scoring at or near the top on exams and asking penetrating questions during that semester. Near the end of the term, he took me aside after class.

"I won't be taking the next semester," he said.

"Why?" I asked, knowing that it would be required for his major.

"Because the next semester covers evolution and, for me, listening to lectures about evolution would be like looking at pornography. I can't do that."

I was stunned. Robert saw the Darwinian model as a deep conflict with his Christian faith. He would not accept my reassurances that the science itself was not a problem. He wound up changing his major.

The second student—I'll call her Kathy—stood at my office door at the end of the first week of class.

"May I talk to you, Dr. Hewlett? It's about religion."

I always begin the semester by telling the students about myself, including my strong Roman Catholic faith.

"Sure, come on in and sit down."

Her eyes were already beginning to tear up as she lowered herself into a chair.

"I come from a small farming community and I'm here at the university to become a medical doctor. But I'm afraid of the science classes I have to take. My father is convinced that I'll lose my faith. What can I do?"

Her question precipitated a long mentoring relationship between us. I prepared a reading list for her, loaning her books from my collection, such as Ken Miller's *Finding*

Darwin's God and John Haught's *God After Darwin*. I set up a schedule where she would see me on a regular basis during my class and, more importantly, during the second semester of the intro course. As a result, she not only persisted in her biology major, but is currently finishing medical school. We communicate now by e-mail and she assures me that everything is fine, both with her science and with her faith.

Those Evening Phone Calls! Teachers Caught in the Crossfire

High school science teachers say that they tremble a bit when the telephone rings in the evening. They fear that it might be one more of "those calls." Those calls come from parents of children who want to know what they're teaching. If the parent is angry at the godless atheists who are trying to secularize our country and take away our Christian heritage, that anger can get displaced onto the teacher at the other end of the phone. It can spoil a teacher's quiet evening at home. Worse, it can cause worry about that teacher's eternal salvation.

Ken Miller testified as an expert witness during the 2005 trial that took place in Harrisburg, Pennsylvania, over the teaching of evolution in the Dover, Pennsylvania, school district. Miller had written a widely used high school textbook on biology. He is also a devout Christian. The day following his testimony, he received five e-mails telling him that he was "going to burn in hell." [1]

University of Kansas Religious Studies Professor Paul Mirecki planned to teach a course, "Special Topics in Religion: Intelligent Design, Creationism and Other Religious Mythologies." He canceled the class after a furor of e-mails complaining that the professor was mocking Christian fundamentalists. It got worse. While driving one evening on a rural road in December 2005, he was tailgated by thugs. They stopped the professor, dragged him from his car, and beat him on the head, back, and shoulders with their fists, punishing him for the class, they said. [2]

We ask: where are the preachers and pastors in this situation? Are the parents who make the frightening phone calls also parents of children in congregations? Has something taken place in church that now comes to expression in the form of displaced anger against schoolteachers and college professors? Does the anger boil and bubble in the churches and then spill over into the public arena, into our schools, before school boards, and before our legislatures? Yes, this appears to be what is happening. It's one more battle in the culture wars, and the combatants include parents.

What about pastors and church leaders? Are the pastors the generals leading their congregations into battle? What happens to the children when they watch the war taking place around their education, even at church? One thing we can note right away. Some end up in Marty's university level biology classes with the painful internal struggles he reports.

The Crisis Breeds Fear

Our society is facing a crisis regarding what to teach the children in our public schools, Roman Catholic parochial schools, evangelical Christian day schools, home schools, along with our colleges and universities. Even more important, our young people are facing a crisis of faith. Many are frightened that what we study in science may

> We believe in courage, and we believe that faith armed with courage is just what God needs from people in our churches today and tomorrow.

threaten our faith. Science may draw us away from belief in God. And because of this fear, some of our young people are steering themselves away from opportunities for a meaningful vocation in science.

What Is at Stake

While many fear that science will undermine faith, we the coauthors of this book have quite a different concern. We fear that a misunderstanding about our faith might create an unnecessary deafness to a divine call to study God's creation through the eyes of the microscope and telescope. What is at stake is the understanding that the world God has made is complex and magnificent; and science provides the lenses through which we can view the fingerprints and footprints left by God's history with our beautiful world. While recognizing that materialistic ideological smudges are occasionally left on the scientific lenses, we believe in taking a look through them anyway—better partial sight than ignorance. We believe in courage, and we believe that faith armed with courage, is just what God needs from people in our churches today and tomorrow.

> We ask for a faith that trusts the truth, knowing that any truth—whether scientific truth or religious truth—must come ultimately from God.

As we face the crisis over evolution, we need a faith that seeks understanding. We ask for *fides quaerens intellectum* ("faith seeking understanding"), in the words of St. Anselm of Canterbury. We ask for a faith that is mature enough to pause and get the facts right before jumping to conclusions. We ask for an unanxious faith that exhibits confidence in the face of ambiguity and difficulty. We ask for a faith that trusts the truth, knowing that any truth—whether scientific truth or religious truth—must come ultimately from God. We ask for a faith that sees itself as a seed, a seed willing to grow, blossom, and expand—a faith that is willing to deepen and enjoy the searchable as well as the unsearchable riches that God has placed before us.

A Map Through the Wilderness of Controversy

It's easy to get lost in the wilderness of the evolution controversy. Is there only one authentic Christian view of evolution? If we get it wrong, do we betray our faith? Must one be an atheist to be a Darwinist? If our ancestors were monkeys, do we lose our dignity? Should public schools silence the Christian voice in favor of a secular view of evolution? Would evangelical day schools and Roman Catholic parochial schools along with families who home school risk contaminating the faith of our children by teaching the "e" word?

What we need is a map. We find ourselves in a wilderness of controversy, and we need a map to find our way through it and onto higher and clearer ground. Such a map is what this book will try to provide.

The road we will follow will begin in a valley and climb to the top of a large hill, making numerous stops along the way. Our point of departure will be the classic Christian faith, the one that derives from the Bible. Roman Catholics, Eastern Orthodox, Evangelical Protestants, and many Liberal Protestants share this classic commitment. As we wind our way up the road, we will pass *evolutionary science* and proceed on toward the atheistic ideologies that some have chosen to build on top of the science, what some have called *atheistic materialism*. We will pause to show respect to the laboratory researchers and the high school teachers who merely want to go to work each day and make a positive contribution to our life together. We will then follow the road up to where *scientific creationism* and *Intelligent Design* reside, where religious soldiers are strategizing for what they believe to be a better science. Beyond this point we will visit with the *theistic evolutionists*, those who believe they can affirm both their Christian faith and evolutionary science as secular scientists present it. Finally, we will arrive at our destination, the hilltop, from which we hope to gain a comprehensive perspective on the road we will have just traveled. On the hilltop, we will try to frame this perspective with a Christian vision informed and even edified by solid science and a larger appreciation of the grandeur of God's creation and God's promise of a new creation.

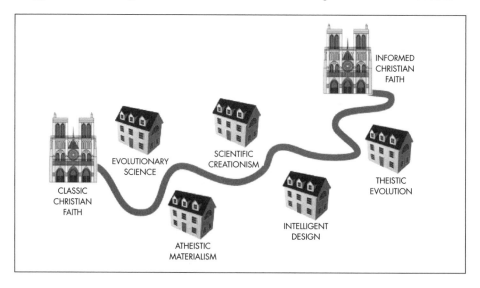

Once we've arrived at the hilltop and look back at our passage, we might want to redraw the map. This is a conceptual map, actually, a spectrum of views. At one end we would place those views according to which God acts directly and perceptibly in natural events. Here God is an interventionist, and we can see the results of God's action in nature. On this end of the spectrum we would place *scientific creationism* and *Intelligent Design* (ID). Creationism holds that God acts decisively at the beginning, at creation. The ID school holds that God acts periodically along the path of evolution, intervening with new designs and jumps in complexity.

At the other end of our spectrum we locate those views in which God is not perceived as an actor in natural processes. Atheists represent this position well, because they believe there is no God who could act. The particular atheists we have in mind here are those who rely specifically on Charles Darwin's theory of evolution. We prefer to call them *ontological materialists*, meaning that they want to say that nothing but the material world has being. They are also known as *reductionists* or *secular humanists*.[3]

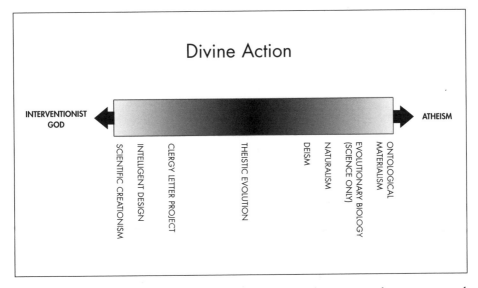

One of the concerns we have is that too frequently these materialists are equated with all practicing scientists, or even the high school teachers of evolution. This is not only a mistake; it is unfair. The average laboratory scientist and typical schoolteacher think of themselves as pursuing science, not as pursuing a materialist ideology, let alone atheism. Even though the scientific method does not make room for transcendental causes, the actual scientists themselves are not necessarily committed to an ideology of materialism. In fact, many are devout Christians. Some are devout Jews or

> It is possible to both believe in God and employ Darwinian evolution as a scientific theory.

Muslims as well. Let us make this point: it is possible to both believe in God and employ Darwinian evolution as a scientific theory.

Marty is a practicing scientist, as we reported earlier. In a lengthy career at a university with a medical school, he has investigated viruses in his laboratory. He's coauthored three editions of a textbook on virology.[4] He knows from extensive experience what good science requires if research is to lead to new knowledge. He finds Darwin's theory of evolution indispensable for learning more about molecular biology and producing the kind of scientific knowledge that could lead to advances in medical therapy. Marty wants no part of ontological materialism, let alone atheism. He wants good science, and good science alone.

One short step toward the middle from the noninterventionist end of the spectrum finds naturalism and deism. In both cases, the natural world has a sense of the sacred about it. In the case of *naturalism*, the world's sacredness is due to the intrinsic value of nature, not to the creative work of a transcendent deity. In the case of *deism*, a transcendent God is responsible for the creation, but that God has now departed and left the world to operate according to the laws of nature. Science studies the laws of nature, while the God who created those laws becomes invisible.

As we move further toward the middle of the spectrum, we find the *theistic evolutionists*. We did not name this group of people. Rather, the name was invented by the scientific creationists as a disparaging title. We fished around for a better title, but we couldn't find one. So, we elected to simply fall in-line and use this term. Within this term, we place a wide spectrum of differing views; but they all have one theme in common: the Christian faith is compatible with the Darwinian interpretation of evolution.

A recent study sponsored by the Episcopal Church in the United States of America, *A Catechism of Creation*, articulates a variant of theistic evolution nicely. "In this evolving universe, God does not dictate the outcome of nature's activities, but allows the world to become what it is able to become in all of its diversity: one could say that God has a purpose rather than a fixed plan, a goal rather than a blueprint." It frames such affirmations within a complementary approach to science and faith. "Science and Christian theology can complement one another in the quest for truth and understanding."[5]

What Do We Advocate?

When we conclude this book, you will find that we would place ourselves in this middle position, subscribing both to Christian faith while embracing the value of the Darwinian model of evolution for scientific research and classroom teaching. In the meantime, we wish to provide an empathetic understanding and explication of the views held by the creationists and the Intelligent Design advocates.

Further, we are earnestly concerned about what this controversy might be doing to young people in our churches and our schools. We fear that they will become discouraged, or worse, fearful about pursuing a life career in science. We believe science is better than television or video games because it provides a window into the natural world. Once we peer through that window, a vast array of depth and breadth and beauty and magnificence opens up. To look through the window science provides opens our eyes to see the grandeur of God's creation as nothing else can.

In addition, the practical advantage of good science is that it leads to technology. Technology in general and medical technology in particular has the potential for improving human health and well-being.

So, to bombard our young people with shock and awe over the evolution controversy may unnecessarily cut them off from many opportunities, one of which is considering science as itself a Christian vocation. It is our earnest desire that young people in middle school and high school are taught the very best science, and this includes the Darwinian model of evolution.

The Church's Role

It is our fervent wish that the pastors and congregations who provide instruction in the Christian faith teach a number of things: first, to trust God before human ideas, and that evolution is one of these human ideas; second, to trust that new knowledge to be gained from a scientific understanding of our world will only enhance our appreciation for God's creation; and third, to trust that faith will provide the courage to consider the possibility that God might be calling us to a vocation either as a scientist or as a supporter of the best science for our society.

What should we teach in our schools, both public and Christian schools? It is our sincere desire that young people in middle school and high school are taught the very best science, and this includes the Darwinian model of evolution. We believe this is serious business. The Darwinian model does much more than just tell us a story about the history of the development of different species on our planet. It provides a model for the study of biology that is progressive for new scientific directions. New research in biology leads to advances in medical science, and this leads to therapies that save human lives. Teaching anything less than the best science is unethical. Whether we like it or not, the Darwinian model is the best science at this point in time.

> Darwinian evolution is a scientific model that provides a fertile research tool leading to new discoveries for biology.

We believe that creationists and Intelligent Design advocates who ask that our school system avoid indoctrinating our young people with materialist atheism have a legitimate concern. Our schools should not teach atheism.

However, a colossal risk of misunderstanding arises when this rightful protest is lifted up. The risk is that the "Christian" view will become associated with the anti-Darwinian views, such as Scientific Creationism or Intelligent Design. The two authors of this book want to emphasize that the Christian faith does not rise or fall with the success or failure of these alternatives to Darwinism. We want to avoid this mistake.

It is possible for a committed Christian to support the teaching of the Darwinian model of evolution. We dare not limit the spectrum of conscientious Christian views to the anti-Darwinians. Acceptance of the science of the Darwinian model can be perfectly consistent with fundamental Christian commitments regarding God as Creator and Christ as Redeemer.[6]

We could imagine a situation in a public school, parochial school, or Christian day school, in which we cautiously teach the controversy. We could imagine a science teacher prefacing a unit in biology by taking the time to alert students to the philosophical and religious interpretations that arise as a result of the science of evolution. We could imagine a teacher offering a brief exposition of atheistic materialism, scientific creationism, Intelligent Design, and theistic evolution. It would be explained that these positions are not, in and of themselves, science, but are philosophical or religious in nature. Once these interpretations have been outlined, the teacher would proceed to teach biology according to the latest and best findings of the field, giving the students the best science the teacher knows of.

Key here in teaching the controversy is to assure students that the label "Christian" is not the exclusive property of the anti-Darwinians, and the label "atheist" is not a necessary result of being a pro-Darwinian. It is possible, the teacher should say, to be both devoutly Christian and a person who celebrates the natural world as seen through the lenses of the original Darwinian and neo-Darwinian models of evolution. In this way, the teacher would start by removing the shrink-wrapping of ideologies that covers up the true science of biological evolution.

CHAPTER TWO

WHAT DID CHARLES DARWIN ACTUALLY SAY?

It would not surprise us to learn that many of our readers are convinced that Charles Darwin wrote, in *Origin of Species*, that God does not exist. This is not the case, however. Yet, Darwin does mention religious belief in his great work. Here, from the definitive 6th and final edition, is what he actually said:

> I see no good reasons why the views given in this volume should shock the religious feelings of any one. It is satisfactory, as showing how transient such impressions are, to remember that the greatest discovery ever made by man, namely, the law of the attraction of gravity, was also attacked by Leibnitz, "as subversive of natural, and inferentially of revealed, religion." A celebrated author and divine has written to me that "he has gradually learned to see that it is just as noble a conception of the Deity to believe that He created a few original forms capable of self-development into other and needful forms, as to believe that He required a fresh act of creation to supply the voids caused by the action of His laws." [1]

Darwin himself shows that his theory of evolution can be compatible with a theological account of creation. Darwin mounted this defense of his theory against religious objections after his original publication had already, in the late 19th century, generated a good deal of controversy. Some were accusing the evolutionary idea of survival of the fittest as undercutting the care for the poor and disadvantaged in society. Some were accusing Darwinism of spreading atheism. We can see from this controversy already within Darwin's own lifetime that evolutionary theory came shrink-wrapped with social and theological implications. But is this warranted? Are these nonscientific applications to religion or society a necessary part of the evolutionary model?

We believe not. We believe that a scientist can pursue laboratory research without the threat of religious bias. And we believe science teachers can teach the Darwinian model of evolution without indoctrinating children with atheism.

Just What Did Charles Darwin Think?

Darwin began his observations of the natural world as a young student, first at the University of Edinburgh in Scotland, and then later at the University of Cambridge in England. In spite of his early attempts at medicine and later his intention to become an ordained minister, he could not separate himself from his attraction to living things. During the spring term of his third year he met the Cambridge botanist Dr. John Henslow. Professor Henslow worked with Darwin as a tutor in mathematics and theology. However, the true influence of their association began when Charles attended Henslow's lectures in botany. This further inspired his calling to the natural sciences, in general, and to his study of the biological world in particular.

In fact, it was Professor Henslow who was instrumental in the offer to Charles Darwin to be the naturalist aboard the British survey ship, H.M.S. *Beagle*, which set sail from Plymouth on December 27, 1831, for a trip around the globe. Darwin would be gone from England for five years.

It was during this voyage that Darwin made the observations and collected the data that would later be used to construct his theory. However, he did not return from the trip with his thoughts completely formed about the evolutionary model. In fact, it was not until his time in London and later in the countryside of Kent that he began to think about what he had seen.

He was greatly influenced by the ideas of other scientists of his times. The geology of Charles Lyell and others convinced him that the age of the Earth was quite old. In addition, Lyell connected him with other naturalists (as biologists were then called) who could help him with the characterization of the many specimens, both modern and fossil, he had brought back on the *Beagle*. Critical to the model he would build were the writings of Thomas Malthus, the British economist who held that populations reproduce so that they eventually outstrip their resources, causing a competition for survival.

Darwin worked on his ideas and his evolutionary model for more than twenty years before finally publishing *The Origin of Species by Means of Natural Selection* in November of 1859. The publication was precipitated by the work of another naturalist, Alfred Wallace, who came to the same conclusions from his studies in South America and Southeast Asia.

What Exactly Does Darwin's Theory Say?

What exactly does Darwin's theory say? A simple statement of it would be that, over millions of years of time, all living creatures on the planet arose by gradual modification from a common ancestor. This so-called descent with modification happened through a process of natural selection.

Darwin used the phrase *natural selection* in direct comparison to the methods of plant and animal breeders. When someone wants to have a sheep that produces better and larger amounts of wool, or corn that tastes sweeter, then selective breeding is employed. In this way, the rancher or farmer encourages those animals or plants that have the desired features to reproduce and prevents those without these features from producing offspring. Darwin called this *artificial selection* and then argued that, in nature, the same kind of thing happens.

For the modern scientist, this theory means that the physical description of life on Earth can best be understood by this model. The data that have been collected, from the fossil record to the study of genes in various animals and plants, all are explained by this idea. Scientists say that the data support the model. We'll have more to say about what this really means in the next chapter when we discuss what a theory is and what scientific models are.

Just How Does Random Variation and Natural Selection Work?

Let's examine Darwinian evolution in a bit more detail. The late biologist John Maynard Smith summarized the evolutionary model in a nice set of points, to which we refer in our first book, *Evolution from Creation to New Creation*. We'll paraphrase those points here.

Imagine a population of creatures, say, a herd of deer. First, the deer can reproduce and multiply. A pair of deer can produce several offspring and the population size will increase. Eventually, such a population could outstrip its resources. Second, not all of the deer are alike. That is, when we look at the herd we can see individual variations in the members. These variations are random differences. Third, when the deer reproduce, a given pair will most often produce offspring with characteristics like the parents. This is called *heredity*.

Now, consider for a minute this herd of deer, reproducing with limited resources. Many will die, some before producing babies. It was apparent to Darwin that some individuals might possess inherited variations that allowed them a greater likelihood of surviving and producing offspring. We could therefore say that these individuals would be more reproductively fit.

Over time, then, the population of deer will change such that more individuals with the advantageous variations would be produced. This takes place because the conditions of the environment select for those traits as opposed to the ones that decrease the reproductive fitness of individual deer. This change over time is what we mean by the word *evolution*.

With the passage of time, the population of deer changes so that these beneficial traits that positively influence reproductive fitness are more represented. This is ultimately what Darwin meant when he added the phrase "survival of the fittest" to later editions of his book. (The phrase, by the way, was not coined by Darwin, but rather by Herbert Spencer, the economist. Darwin just thought that the phrase described what he had been trying to say.)

This description of the deer herd describes what Darwin understood to be "descent with modification through natural selection."

Darwin came to this model by observing the fossilized remains of species that no longer existed, as well as by looking at current species, such as the famous finches on the Galapagos Islands. He also proposed that, over the vast geologic time periods that were just then coming to be understood, these kinds of changes would eventually lead to the production of new species.

The word *species* is important here. A species is defined in one sense by what is called *reproductive isolation*. This means that members of one species cannot reproduce with members of another species. The Darwinian model predicts that such species arise over periods of time (again, by this we mean geological time scales) when variations are selected such that members of a population can no longer reproduce with one another. This is called *speciation*. This might happen, for instance, when populations of organisms get separated by geography. In these cases, with the passage of time, speciation would take place.

Another important set of terms that we will come to later are *microevolution* and *macroevolution*. By microevolution, we mean the changes that take place over time within a species; things like subtle changes in the structure of the beaks of birds. *Macroevolution* means that the changes actually lead to speciation, the development of new species. We will see that this becomes important in the view of the Scientific Creationists.

The Neo-Darwinian Synthesis

During the twentieth century, the Darwinian model was joined with the new understanding of genes, heredity, and mutations to make what is now called the neo-Darwinian synthesis. Darwin, of course, knew nothing of genes or DNA. In fact, Gregor Mendel, the Augustinian monk working in Austria, published his work on pea plants just nine years after *Origin of Species* appeared. However, the scientific world would take some fifty years to accept the principles of heredity that Mendel described.

Combining the rules of genetics with the discoveries of DNA and the functioning of genes as molecules would lead to an understanding of evolution at the cellular and even molecular level. In this view, the variations in the deer population, for example, are spoken of as slight changes in the DNA code. It also becomes clear that these changes occur in ways that cannot be predicted. The word *random* is used to describe this. The changes are really unpredictable, even though they take place based on the regular or lawlike behavior of the molecules. This means that even though we know how the DNA changes, we cannot predict what will be changed in a particular mutation or variation event.

When we use terms such as *Darwinism* or the *Darwinian model*, we include the entire Darwinian tradition, Darwin's original theory combined with the more recent neo-Darwinian synthesis of random genetic variation with natural selection. Even this stage of neo-Darwinism is becoming almost outdated, as new discoveries require extensions of the original model. We are already in a post neo-Darwinian period. Be that as it may, what the controversy is about is the single unbroken tradition within science that begins with Charles Darwin and runs through the present framework for pursuing evolutionary biology.

That summarizes the science of biological evolution, unpackaged from all of the social and theological implications with which it has been wrapped. Why, then, is this so controversial in some quarters? After all, isn't this just an example of science doing what science does, attempting to derive physical explanations for physical features of the natural world?

Of course, when Darwin sailed away on the *Beagle*, he was as convinced as were most Englishmen of his day that the creation story as told in Genesis 1:1–2:4a was, in fact, a fairly accurate description of what happened. That is not to say that he was a Biblical literalist. But this does mean that he accepted the notion that most of what we see in the world was created by God pretty much in the form in which we see it. It was the nature of the scientific age, however, to challenge such convictions; and Darwin was a product of his day.

What Did Darwinism Do to Belief in God?

Immediately upon publication of *Origin of Species* in 1859, social and theological interpretations and challenges seemed to get out of control. One of Darwin's friends,

Herbert Spencer, whom we mentioned earlier, championed the idea that social systems and governments were also subject to natural selection. His view, therefore, was that we ought to let things proceed such that the best system is selected and the less fit ones die out—his *laissez-faire* capitalism of the late nineteenth century. To create a naturalistic ethic based on survival of the fittest would mean leaving the poor and infirm in society to die by the roadside. This could not be reconciled with a Christian ethic or a Christian conscience. Spencer's ideas gave birth to what we now know as social Darwinism, an anathema to Christian ethics.

Thomas Huxley, another friend of both Darwin and Spencer, went even further. He proposed the development of a secular religion based on evolution, rejecting notions of God and traditional religious thought altogether. For Huxley and his followers, Darwin's biology provided scientific justification for materialism, and therefore, ontological atheism. Huxley could embrace atheism, but he did not endorse Spencer's heartless social ethics. He thought his new evolutionary view of religion could lead us to a more caring society than "survival of the fittest" would dictate. Huxley believed that some humans were at a point where they could free themselves from the enslavement of religion. This is important to note, because it is not the atheism that generates the ruthless ethic of social Darwinism.

Another partner in these discussions was Darwin's friend and cousin, Francis Galton. Galton thought that modern society could deliberately speed up evolution toward fitter families through planned breeding. He began the program we now know as *eugenics*. The practice of eugenics was thought to be progressive and liberal; so it spread quickly and widely. In England and the United States, *positive eugenics* encouraged the "better" families to have more children. In *negative eugenics*, prisoners, paupers, and mentally retarded people were sterilized to prevent them having children. In Germany, both positive and negative eugenics were carried to the extreme. Galton's version of Darwinism inspired the Nazi program of "racial hygiene," which led to government-run breeding programs with selected Aryan men and women, and the gas chamber deaths of the mentally retarded, physically handicapped, homosexual, Gypsies, and Jews. Selective breeding and the mass elimination of those deemed unfit to survive could speed up the evolutionary advance of the human race.

From the earliest discussions, then, Darwin's model of evolution has been associated with a formidable challenge to traditional understandings of society and relationship with the Divine. We will see in a later chapter how this has unfolded over time and is present in the discussions today.

As for Darwin himself, he was not immune to the implications of his model for his own belief system. While he never became the atheist that some of his champions would have liked to see, he was, by the end of his life, quite agnostic. Two things seem to have influenced this change from the minister-to-be who studied at Cambridge.

First, the implications of his model for the way in which nature works to select some and reject others seems to be cruel. Virtually all life needs to destroy life in order to live. Darwin described the suffering in nature and the loss to extinction of 90 percent of species as "waste." How can one justify a God who would allow such cruelty and waste in creation? Either such a God is powerless to stop this, or is, in fact, allowing it by design. Darwin raised this issue on more than one occasion, with reference to how natural selection works over time.

Second, and perhaps more important in his life, was the tragic death of his daughter, Anne Elizabeth, of tuberculosis in 1851 at the age of ten. He grieved deeply. This event changed Darwin's personal religious outlook and may have had a great deal to do with how he viewed the nonscientific implications of his model.

We want to emphasize once more that Darwinian evolution is an explanatory theory or model based on observations. That is to say, it is a specific view of the natural world developed by the very human activity we call science. In the next chapter we'll see how scientists work and what their enterprise is set up to produce.

CHAPTER THREE

ONLY A THEORY? WHAT DO RESEARCH SCIENTISTS ACTUALLY DO?

We said to begin with that the science we do must be the best, must be fertile, and must lead us to new knowledge that is productive for our society. When Marty sets out to train the physicians of tomorrow in his classes, he needs to provide them the tools of a science that will allow them to give us the best medical care that they can.

> The science we do must be the best, must be fertile, and must lead us to new knowledge that is productive for our society.

Do you know a research scientist? There are probably fewer than 800,000 people holding doctoral degrees in science and engineering in the U.S. today. With our population of nearly 145 million adults, your chances of knowing one of these researchers is not very high. Still, in some communities with large universities there's a reasonable probability that you have an acquaintance who is involved in research.

If you do know a scientist, have you ever asked her or him what it is she or he does? Do you know how a scientist thinks about his or her work? What is it exactly that these 800,000 people do?

When Did All of This Start?

The modern enterprise that we call science began with the Enlightenment, whose roots can be found in the 14th and 15th centuries and formative development in the 16th, 17th and 18th centuries. It was then that people began to emphasize the role of reason. This rise of reason influenced the way Western Europe viewed the natural world. Galileo, Descartes, Newton, Pascal, and others developed the logical thought processes necessary to describe physical aspects of nature in a reproducible fashion—what we now call the *scientific method*. The early versions of what was called natural philosophy did not truly resemble the modern scientific enterprise, except in the reliance on a method of procedure. It was not really until the 18th century that what we have come to know as "*science*" assumed its present shape.

And just what is this human activity? Science is, at its heart, a very specific way of seeing the world. It models the world. It is a point of view. In order to achieve this particular view, science employs a method, a specific way of doing things. When the French mathematician and philosopher, René Descartes, separated his world into his mind (his "thinking thing") and everything else ("the extended thing"), he precipitated a philosophical shift that had good points and bad points. On the good side, his insight allowed the development of a systematic approach to asking questions about what we observe. On the bad side, he created a rift between the physical and the spiritual that has become part of the very problem we are discussing now. He separated subjects and objects. He separated our subjective minds from the material objects we observe. This Cartesian split, as it is called, is now synonymous with what philosophers call *substance dualism*; and our generation finds it difficult to put back together the body and the soul, the material and the spiritual.

Darwinism is a child of substance dualism, according to which living creatures are seen as material objects of study and research. This is why scientific Darwinism appears to be devoid of spirit or soul.

What Is the Scientific Method?

Now, let's look in more detail at the method that descended from Descartes with modification, or, as it is called, the scientific method. Here is a typical scenario. A scientist first begins with an objective observation of something in the natural world—it might be a change in the condition of a gas with heating or cooling. He or she notices something that seems remarkable, something that needs further exploration. The scientist makes measurements of the phenomenon and collects these data. The second step is to formulate a hypothesis that might explain the observations. Notice that this step requires that the observations be repeatable, that is, that the scientist can observe many more than one occurrence of the phenomenon. Please note the importance of repeating observations.

The third step is critical in the method, in that it requires the scientist to design experimental tests of the hypothesis. The fundamental nature of the scientific hypothesis is that it should make predictions of the outcome of these experimental tests. If any of the tests fail, then the hypothesis may be invalid. Science does not attempt to prove the validity of hypotheses, but rather attempts to falsify them. This experimental testing is repeated and the explanatory hypothesis revised as needed.

The final stage of the method takes place when, after sufficient tests, the hypothesis seems to be holding up. In this case, science might call the explanatory model a theory. If sufficient tests of the theory fail to invalidate it, over time it might be called a law. There are only a few such laws in science, such as the law of gravity or the laws of thermodynamics in physics, or the laws of genetics in biology.

What Is a Scientific Theory?

The fact that something is called a "theory" rather than a "law" should be understood very carefully. The word *"theory"* is used outside of science in a much different way. In common usage, something that is theoretical is often thought to be synonymous with "imaginary" or "unproven." However, in science, a theory is a way of organizing facts and is tested over and over again. A good theory is one that has not yet been falsified, proved false. The Darwinian theory has not yet been falsified, despite what some people say.

This is an important distinction, and one that is clouded in the debates concerning evolution. This confusion was evident in the 2004 Cobb County, Georgia, case involving stickers placed on high school biology texts, calling evolution "a theory, not a fact." The actual situation is that, in science, theories are supported by facts, in the form of data and experiment. The facts supporting the Darwinian model are so numerous no one can count them. In summary, it is the case that the Darwinian model is a theory, but this does not imply any scientific weakness.

> A theory is a way of organizing facts and is tested over and over again.

How Is the Darwinian Model of Evolution a Science?

Darwinian evolution is different from other sciences in one sense. Evolution happens over epochs of time. In addition, we say that the process of evolution is "contingent." This means that the results we observe depend to a great extent on the conditions under which natural selection operates. As a result, if we rewind and then replay the tape of evolution, as the late Stephen Jay Gould was fond of saying, we would not get the same result. Another way of saying this is that the data we have for evolution are historical in nature. History cannot easily be replicated in the laboratory.

This is not to say that some things about evolution cannot be tested in the laboratory. Certainly, natural selection itself can be demonstrated, both in the laboratory as well as in nature. The difficult part is seeing the results of this over long enough time to reap the fruits of evolution, especially the development of new species. Some experiments are beginning to provide evidence for this. But we can get a hint of this when we say that certain disease-producing populations become resistant to a particular medicine. This resistance is due, in large part, to the process of natural selection.

Now, does this mean that the science of evolution is not sound? On the contrary, the theory of evolution is supported by a wide variety of types of data, from the fossil record to analysis of the structure of proteins that make up all living systems. The theory has not been falsified as yet by any of the observations. In fact, the theory allows predictions to be made about the outcome of experiments and, in each case, the outcome confirms rather than invalidates the theory.

Science Gives Us *Models*, Not the Whole Truth

We have also been using the word *model* with respect to evolution. This word needs further explanation. Science, as we have mentioned, works with phenomena in the natural world that are regular or repeatable. The explanatory hypothesis that is derived after observations such as these is sometimes called a model. This is in recognition of the fact that the hypothesis or theory is a best attempt to explain what has been observed.

In some sense, the model is a working structure. Models have utility in that they have *explanatory power* and *predictive power* (fertility). In addition, models must be *testable* and subject to possible falsification. A model must meet all three of these criteria to be considered a valid scientific model. We also have a sense that our model somehow approximates reality. Note here that we say "approximates reality." We do not view a scientific model as absolute truth. Rather, a model provides a conceptual structure that directs and guides future research and leads to new knowledge.

> Models have *explanatory power* and *predictive power.*

A good model generates hypotheses for further research—it is fertile or fruitful. The Darwinian model of evolution inspires paleontologists to dig up fossils and artifacts and create time lines for natural history. It prompts primatologists to observe chimpanzee social behavior over generations to see exactly how reproductive fitness is accomplished.

The neo-Darwinian model inspires geneticists to examine DNA in many species, looking for commonalities that could indicate a shared history over time. So-called human "junk DNA" seems to contain certain information found in former viruses, so future research into junk DNA may eventually tell us more about the prehistoric migratory patterns of our ancestors. More important, random variations in genomes due to mutations, as well as our coevolution with viruses, have enormous implications for diagnosing genetic diseases and developing pharmaceuticals.

At any point in fossil gathering, observing species, or examining DNA, evidence may appear that would modify or even falsify the larger Darwinian model with which research began. On the one hand, the model inspires new research. On the other hand, new research constantly puts the model to the test. This is why scientific knowledge is growing—even evolving, we might say.

What Does It Mean to Be an Objective Observer?

What do we mean when we say "objective observer"? This is often confusing, for both the scientist and the nonscientist. Many who work at the discipline of science believe that the data they gather in pursuit of the falsification of a particular hypothesis are, in fact, objective. Dictionary definitions of this word include such statements as "having actual existence or reality" or "presented factually" or "uninfluenced by emotions." The general notion, then, is that the data of science are equivalent to the reality of the world that is being observed.

What many current-day scientists fail to appreciate is that, with the advent of the use of instrumentation to allow observations of things that the eye cannot see by itself, some of these aspects of objectivity no longer apply. For such situations it might be better to claim that the data are objective so far as the model upon which the observation is built is valid. We prefer to say that the data are "theory-laden," meaning that the observations are in some sense filtered through the lens of the hypothesis or theory that is being used.

Now, before you run off and shout "Marty and Ted have just said that all science is invalid because data are theory-laden," let's take a hard look at what this all means. The central feature of the scientific enterprise is falsification. This means that all theories or even laws are always subject to experimental testing. At any time in science, existing paradigms can be overturned and new paradigms set in place that change interpretations of data. This can even change the kinds of data that are collected, as new instruments are designed based on the new paradigms.

Thomas Kuhn, the influential philosopher and historian of science in the mid-20th century, argued that such revolutions in paradigm are, in fact, the way that science progresses to new views. We've seen many examples of this, including the change from the earth-centric model of Ptolemy to the sun-centric model of Copernicus, or the change from Newtonian physics to quantum physics. Our general idea is that we will continue to see this kind of revolutionary change. Science is open to such change and our scientific understanding of the world requires such change. So, don't be alarmed that we've said that data are theory-laden. They're supposed to be! That's part of how science works.[1]

Charles Darwin was using his eyes as instruments of observation and therefore was less subject to this issue. Nonetheless, he was working within the prevailing paradigms of science in the 19th century. In the next chapter, we'll explore what those paradigms were, how they've changed, and how some scientists slide over from using the paradigms as method to using the paradigms as philosophy.

Darwin's World and Ours

Before we leave this discussion of what scientists actually do, let's consider Darwin the man. He walked this earth just as we all do, experiencing the wonders of creation with his senses. He was an observer, in the same way that every living thing observes or interacts with the world. It isn't that reality was somehow different for Darwin than it is for you. It was the same reality, displaced in time by about 170 years. The world that Darwin recorded during his five-year voyage on the *Beagle* was the same world that Gregor Mendel tinkered with in his pea garden in Brün, Austria. It was the same world from which James Watson and Francis Crick extracted the information that allowed them to build a model of DNA. And of course, it was the same world in which St. Augustine lived and taught, in which St. Thomas Aquinas moved and thought, in which Martin Luther had his great insights about faith, and from which all of us will move on some day. And, it goes without saying, this is the world that Christ entered through the incarnation and then redeemed with his ultimate atonement on the cross that day at Calvary.

What does this have to do with scientists and their activity? Just that we all live in and experience the same reality. It is our reaction to that reality that differs. The scientific response to that reality is one that attempts to come to a certain kind of view, one that is quantifiable, testable, and, in some sense, that is defined by the method as objective. But it is still, at its heart, a response to experience. The responses of Augustine, Aquinas, and Luther are no more or no less a human reaction to creation. -

CAN WE BELIEVE IN GOD AND EVOLUTION?

So, if we're correct and science is simply a method for describing a quantitative view of the world that results in testable models, how did everyone get into this mess over evolution? What's the problem?

Confusing Science and Philosophy

We often talk with scientists and ask them about their philosophical positions. An all too common response is "I don't have a philosophy." We, of course, point out that not having a philosophy is, in fact, a philosophy!

But, more to the point, the scientific enterprise does have a philosophical base, a set of assumptions and values that underpin the way work is done. In the previous chapter, we tried to outline the method of science. This method presupposes several things: (a) that order exists in nature, (b) that we can indeed observe this order, and (c) that models can be derived that provide naturalistic explanations for observed ordered phenomena. All of this is so that the method of science can be concerned exclusively with the physical world, that is, with Descartes' "everything other than mind/spirit." There is nothing in this philosophical decision that precludes or excludes the existence of the nonphysical or the supernatural. This decision comes out of prior decisions by scientists about how to proceed, their method or approach.

Modern science has made another methodological choice. It is easier to design experiments if you focus on the pieces of the phenomenon rather than if you focus on the complex whole. For instance, if you want to understand a cell in a frog, it is relatively easy to take the cell apart and study the pieces that make up the cell. Marty is a biochemist and his training in science has been all about the methods for doing this and the kinds of models that you can build with the data you observe. Philosophers call this process of applying a method to study the cell by isolating its component parts *methodological reductionism*. The main idea here is that science, in order to have a greater understanding of the complex whole, assembles the more basic building blocks that make up the whole. In other words, to understand the whole, you have to first understand its parts.

Now, suppose that you're a scientist, working on the parts of the cell. You have models that explain the behavior of proteins in the cell and even of the genetics of the cell in terms of the DNA found in the nucleus. In fact, the modern structure of biology is built on this kind of understanding of the function of all living things. You might find yourself thinking, "Heh, this is very powerful information. Look what I can do with these models in terms of generating new experiments. You know, maybe the most valid way of understanding a cell is in terms of the parts that make up the cell."

If you make this statement a part of your way of thinking about living systems, you've just made a philosophical, not a scientific choice. What you've done is made a decision about what kind of knowledge is valid with respect to the cell and to all of life. In philosophy, the study of knowledge systems is called *epistemology*. You choose to be an epistemological reductionist. Notice that this is not a scientific conclusion; it cannot be proven false. It has nothing to do with observation, or method, or even theory and model construction. It has to do with a philosophical reaction to the processes and outcomes of science.

Suppose that your work with the parts of the cell leads you to understanding the chemistry and even the physics of these parts. Of course this was your agreed upon purpose all along. But that agreement took place a long time ago and you haven't thought about it in some time. It's easy to see how you might become convinced that the parts of the cell and the atoms of which they are made are really all that there is to living things. You could start to think that the material of the universe is actually all that exists; there is nothing else.

In philosophy, the study of the essence or being of things is called *ontology*. So, at this point you've made the philosophical decision to be an ontological reductionist. Again, this is not a scientific conclusion. Remember our agreement—science should be about the physical world. Therefore, to conclude that the physical is all that exists is very much an error in logic—it's a circular argument. That is, you decided only to look at the physical and then you concluded that that is all there is.

In the process of making these philosophical decisions, it may be that you come to regard the concept of God as superfluous. In fact, since you've become convinced that nothing exists except the material, the next step is to conclude that God does not exist. This conclusion is called atheism. And because you accept only the material as real, you have become an *atheistic materialist*.

Is It Necessary to Be an Atheistic Materialist in Order to Be a Scientist?

The simple answer is "of course not!" After all, Marty is a scientist and he's not an atheistic materialist. We would bet that most scientists, if you asked them, would not identify themselves with this philosophy. Oh, it's true that surveys show a higher percentage of agnostics and atheists among scientists than in the nonscientific population. But this statistic is also true of academia in general.

The real question to address here is, *What step in the scientific method requires the scientist to declare that God does not exist?* If you go back to the previous chapter, you'll see that our method has nothing to do with this. We observe, we hypothesize, we experiment, we revise, we theorize. All of this is done in order to have a model of the natural world that has explanatory and predictive powers. Nothing in this methodology requires any kind of religious commitment, either pro- or anti-God.

In fact, all that's necessary to be a scientist is a curiosity about the natural world and an attraction to the scientific method as a way to understand that world. Scientists, like anyone else, can react to their life experiences and, as a result, have a particular religious and philosophical position. Some scientists might look at their models of nature and conclude that there is no God. Others, looking at the same models, are struck by the wonder and beauty of God's creation.

Atheistic Materialists and the Battle for Our Hearts and Minds

It is obvious from some of the writings and public statements of those who hold the ontological materialist or atheist position that they want everyone to get on board the same train. It is their view that if only society would come around to an atheistic philosophical view, everything would be solved.

To this end they write dramatically that there is only one way of knowing anything real about the universe and only one valid way to think about things. Here are some examples.

First, there is the late Francis Crick, the codeveloper with James Watson of the DNA model that is one of the hallmark icons of modern biology, who wrote: "The ultimate aim of the modern movement in biology is in fact to explain *all* biology in terms of physics and chemistry. . . . Eventually one may hope to have the whole of biology 'explained' in terms of the level below it, and so on right down to the atomic level." [1]

Then there is Richard Dawkins, the Oxford scientist and prolific popularizer of evolutionary biology, who says: "The universe that we observe has precisely the properties we should expect if there is, at bottom, no design, no purpose, no evil and no good, nothing but blind, pitiless indifference." [2]

Next is the Tufts University philosopher Daniel Dennett, who claims: "The prevailing wisdom, variously expressed and argued for, is materialism: there is only one sort of stuff, namely matter the physical stuff of physics, chemistry, and physiology, and the mind is a physical phenomenon." [3]

There are even those, like the Harvard biologist Richard Lewontin, who blatantly admit that this is a specifically chosen point of view: "We have a prior commitment, a commitment to materialism. . . . Materialism is absolute, for we cannot allow a divine foot in the door." [4]

Curiously, the atheistic materialists who see themselves as defending the bulwarks of established science against the assaults of what they consider a superstitious religious fervor are capable of mustering humorous rhetorical weaponry. Daniel Dennett fires a volley at conservative Christians that mimics what he perceives is being fired at his side. The religious right has "mastered the art of refutation by caricature, and pounces on every opportunity to replace cautiously expressed articulations of the evolutionary facts with sensationalized oversimplifications that they can then hoot at and warn the world about." [5] Now, we ask, who's calling the kettle black? We're certainly glad to read that in the heat of rhetorical battle, Dennett avoids "caricature" or "oversimplifications."

Is Science Incompatible with the Religious Viewpoint?

Daniel Dennett is busy fueling the fires of discontent between science and religion. For the life of us, we don't understand why. We are being very specific here in wanting to see science as not having the commitment to materialism that Dennett or Crick or Lewontin claim. Instead, we insist that science is a wonderful human journey to explore the natural world and to build explanatory models that enrich our understanding of that world. We see no need for this to be in any way at odds with our faith in

God. Instead, we see the scientific enterprise as something that should inflame our desire to know God in a deeper way.

In her book *God's Ecstasy*, Beatrice Bruteau writes about why a Christian contemplative needs to understand science. She says: "The conclusion for the religious person should be that the world is God's most personal work, therefore something for us to know and admire and revere, to take part in, to contribute to creating—since it is made as a self-creating universe." [6]

> **The scientific enterprise should inflame our desire to know God in a deeper way.**

Bruteau expresses awe about the natural world as revealed by science. She sees no incompatibility with her Christian faith and that world. In fact, she demands that Christians must be interested in the world as science sees it because that is what God is interested in.

With reference to the evolutionary biology model in particular, Georgetown theologian John Haught writes about "Darwin's gift to theology." He argues that "the central and original content of Christian faith provides us with an image of God that is not only logically consistent with but fruitfully illuminative of the Darwinian picture of life." [7]

This is a pretty strong statement—God as consistent with the Darwinian picture of life? How can this be?

Haught develops his ideas within the framework of his Roman Catholic Christian faith. He tells us that it is God's infinite love that resulted in this creation. The fact that we are still in the process of becoming, still in creation, is central to understanding how evolution fits with this Christian worldview. Haught further argues that God's love is so far-reaching that God allowed his only Son to become a part of this very creation that is still evolving. The incarnation and the suffering of the cross are then seen as crucial to reconciling theology and Darwin. For Haught, accepting evolution with all of its implications is essential for his theological understanding of Christ's redemptive act.

So, our short answer is yes; science and religion are compatible. Even more than that, science and religion have much to say to each other.

CHAPTER FIVE

DOES EVOLUTION CORRUPT OUR VALUES?

Does the concept of evolution corrupt our values? Christian creationists believe it does. John D. Morris, a creationist, writes that he and others are "pointing the finger at naturalistic evolutionary teaching in our schools as the real culprit in teen drug use, the rampant spread of sexually transmitted diseases, despair and suicide in teens as well as youth violence." Not only does evolutionary biology lead to a deterioration of social values, it promotes a godless naturalism in our public schools. Morris objects to "the 'religion' of naturalism masquerading in the name of science, while all support for supernaturalism is censored." [1] Now, just what is behind this? We will briefly review the history to answer this question.

Darwin's Relatives and Friends: Spencer, Galton, and Huxley

When Darwin published his 1859 book *Origin of Species*, it was delivered first to bookstores in Victorian England. Imagine walking into the London equivalent of Borders or Barnes & Noble that late November day and seeing a display that touted "New! From Charles Darwin of the village of Downe! How It All Began!" No Amazon.com here—just foot traffic and customers.

Darwin was relatively unknown, except to a few members of the Royal Society with whom he had been working. In addition, he did not live in London any longer, but, instead, kept mostly to himself at his country estate. Unlike today, when publishers have first printings in the millions, especially for well-known authors, Darwin's first edition appeared as 1,250 copies. It was sold out the day it was issued. The second edition appeared in January of 1860.

Why all of the interest? What was it about this book that demanded that everyone read it? Remember that Darwin's model changed over time and did not reach its present form until almost the middle of the 20th century, when it had been married with genetics and molecular biology to make the modern synthesis. So why not treat it the same way that Gregor Mendel's work had been treated? Why not relegate it to the heap of scientific works that, while carefully conducted and written, had no real impact? The answer is that Darwin's science exploded with social and theological shrapnel. His collegial friends saw to it that evolutionary biology spread into (a) the social Darwinism of Herbert Spencer, (b) the eugenics of Francis Galton, and (c) the agnosticism and atheism of Thomas Huxley. To these three explosive social threats mentioned earlier we now return.

From Biological Darwinism to Social Darwinism

Unlike Mendel's work for which science was not prepared in 1869, Darwin's book encountered a society that was ready to receive it. England at the end of the 19th century had fully embraced the industrial revolution and its role as world power. The "colonies" were still stretching and coming of age, but England saw herself as the intellectual center of the West.

The idea that nature works by selecting the best and the brightest resonated with many scholars in Britain. Herbert Spencer was one of these. Spencer was likely a more influential figure than Darwin in 19th-century England and, for that matter, all of Europe. He was interested in many things and wrote widely on philosophy, science, economics, and social theory. Spencer actually came up with a theory of evolution before Darwin. However, his work did not have the kind of data collection and rigor that Darwin's did and, as a result, we do not speak of Spencerian evolution.

Nonetheless, Spencer was a major force in Victorian Britain. As soon as *Origin of Species* made its appearance, it fit well with the kinds of arguments that Spencer had been making for years. He was a proponent of Adam Smith's *laissez-faire* capitalism. The French phrase used here is a shorter version of a longer phrase *laissez faire, laissez passer*, which means "let things alone, let them pass." Spencer believed that the evolutionary model, whether his or Darwin's, could be applied to societies and governments as well as to species. As a result, he wrote that we ought to simply let governments and economies compete, and the fittest would survive. Remember that this term, *survival of the fittest*, was created by Spencer and later used by Darwin as an equivalent to *natural selection* in the 6th edition of *Origin of Species*.

This idea of the less fit being left alone, to fall by the wayside—applied to economies and countries, or people within economies and countries—does not sit well with our Christian values. After all, Jesus says "Inasmuch as ye have done it unto one of the least of these my brethren, ye have done it unto me" (Matt 25:40). We are charged to take care of the weak and oppressed, to feed the hungry, cloth the naked, give to the poor. How can it be Christian to let them be lost as "unfit"?

Spencer and others were proposing what has come to be called *social Darwinism*. It is one layer of that shrink-wrapping that was applied over the science of evolution practically from the beginning. However, it is not a requirement for evolutionary biology that it be applied to social systems. The data, whether they be found in the fossil record or DNA and protein sequences, have nothing to do with the fitness of the poor. Christian ethics is not modeled on what nature does. Christian ethics derives from the teachings of Jesus and the anticipation of God's redemptive future.

From Darwin to Galton to Eugenics to Genocide

Everyone was reading *Origin of Species*, not the least of whom were members of Darwin's own family. One of these, a cousin named Francis Galton, was another prominent figure of the time. Galton, like Spencer, was a man of many interests. He had been an explorer in Africa, a developer of weather models, a proponent of the use of fingerprinting for criminal investigation, to name only a few. Among his list of accomplishments was the invention of the field of study and practice called *eugenics*.

Galton reasoned that, if his cousin was correct and natural selection resulted in increased fitness, then it only stood to reason that humans could benefit from this idea. He proposed, therefore, that the "best" humans ought to be encouraged to reproduce, thus increasing fitness of the species. We have deliberately placed the word *best* in quotations here, since the definition of what is meant by the "best humans" was certainly questionable.

In Galton's masterwork, *Hereditary Genius*, published ten years after his cousin's book, he writes in the first chapter:

> I propose to show in this book that a man's natural abilities are derived by inheritance, under exactly the same limitations as are the form and physical features of the whole organic world. Consequently, as it is easy, notwithstanding those limitations, to obtain by careful selection a permanent breed of dogs or horses gifted with peculiar powers of running, or of doing anything else, so it would be quite practicable to produce a highly-gifted race of men by judicious marriages during several consecutive generations.[2]

And just who would be encouraged to breed in order to produce this "highly-gifted race?" Why, the British aristocracy, of course. Galton takes great pains in his book to "document" the racial inferiorities of everyone else when compared with the Anglo-Saxon male.

Galton's eugenic proposals were, at least, positive, in that they were designed to encourage certain breeding patterns. When these ideas arrived in America, however, both positive and negative eugenics became the vogue. Not only were the more fit encouraged to breed, but the presumed less fit were discouraged and, in some cases, legally and physically prevented from breeding. Sterilization of so-called mental defectives was practiced in the United States well into the 20th century. And one outcome of the application of eugenic principles, laws prohibiting interracial marriage, were in place in at least 16 states until 1967.

The situation went from bad to worse when eugenics arrived in Germany at the turn of the 20th century. Eugenics became a cultural ideal. Africans were the first to be defined as unfit and subject to genocide; and the German military performed genocide on the Hottentots in Southwest Africa. Later, eugenics and anti-Semitism joined forces to define Jews as unfit for survival.

In the 1920s Adolph Hitler read Darwin, Spencer, and Galton and used evolution to formulate his doctrine of "racial hygiene." Under the Nazis, Hitler intended to advance evolution by eliminating the "unfit" and creating a master race of superior people, the *Übermensch*. To eliminate the unfit the Nazis designed the gas chambers in the late 1930s and placed in them children who were mentally or physically handicapped. After the "final solution" was formulated in 1941, Jews were added to the list of those who would be exterminated in the gas chambers, and a program of state-supported genocide followed. The horror of the Holocaust lives in our collective memory as a legacy of evolution, social Darwinism, eugenics, and genetics applied in the name of racial extremism.

Historically, a component of the shrink-wrapping became the idea that humans could and should weed out the undesirables—the unfit—from their ranks. Again, Jesus weighs in on this question for us when he champions the cause of the weak and powerless, when he does not run from the lepers or the lame, and when he dines with those who seem to be on the lowest rung of the ladder. Jesus gave special attention to those the eugenicists would find unfit. The eugenic manifestos of the early to middle 20th century strike the believing Christian as nothing less than evil.

When creationists and others complain that evolution corrupts social values, this is the history they have in mind. It would be a mistake to dismissingly assume that such critics are merely right-wing homophobes or just plain anti-liberals. The critics of the Darwinian tradition are well aware of the history of wanton bloodshed in the name of a scientifically supported social ethic, a social ethic that must at all points be combated by Christian values such as compassion and justice. Perhaps when these social critics draw a straight line between the public school teaching of Darwinian science to increases in teen suicide and violence, they are egregiously overstating the case; yet, the energy giving rise to this passion derives from a history of murder and violence perpetrated in the name of the survival of the fittest.

And yet, we want to add, *nowhere* in modern evolutionary science does it say that survival of the fittest or eugenics are necessary or desired ethical practices. Social Darwinism is not a part of the scientific model of how all of life is interrelated.

From Darwinism to Agnosticism to Atheism

While the scientific scholars of Victorian England were avidly digesting Darwin's work, the religious debate about its implications was taking form. Even though some of the clerical community could see value in his model, others worried that it diminished the place of humans in creation, making us only one among many other kinds of animals who descended from some common ancestor. The image of humans being related to apes was too much for some to take. And so the criticisms began.

Among the strongest defenders of Darwin was Thomas Huxley, a London physician and scientist. Recall that Darwin's book was published on November 22, 1859. The very next day, Huxley wrote a letter to Darwin in which he said:

> My dear Darwin—I finished your book yesterday, a lucky examination having furnished me with a few hours of continuous leisure.
>
> Since I read Von Bär's essays, nine years ago, no work on Natural History Science I have met with has made so great an impression upon me, and I do most heartily thank you for the great store of new views you have given me. Nothing, I think, can be better than the tone of the book—it impresses those who know about the subject. As for your doctrine, I am prepared to go to the stake. . . .
>
> I trust you will not allow yourself to be in any way disgusted or annoyed by the considerable abuse and misrepresentation which, unless I greatly mistake, is in store for you. Depend upon it, you have earned the lasting gratitude of all thoughtful men. And as to the curs which will bark and yelp, you must recollect that some of your friends, at any rate, are endowed with an amount of combativeness which (though you have often and justly rebuked it) may stand you in good stead.
>
> I am sharpening up my claws and beak in readiness. [3]

Huxley became, by his own description, "Darwin's bulldog," defending evolutionary theory at every chance both in England and abroad. For the rest of his life, until his death in 1895, he would be among the leaders of those intellectuals calling for not just a scientific acceptance of Darwinian evolution, but a virtual remake of society based on its principles. In 1880, the American journal *Science* published the text of a presentation given by Huxley at the Royal Institute. The title of his talk was "The Coming of Age of the Origin of Species," referring to the 21 years since the publication. He began the talk by holding up one of the original 1859 editions of the book. It was clear from his remarks that, for him, Darwin's ideas had become much more than science—they had taken on a religious importance. For instance, in that talk he said:

> It would be a poor way of celebrating the Coming of Age of the Origin of Species were I merely to dwell upon the facts, undoubted and remarkable as they are, of its far-reaching influence and of the great following of ardent disciples who are occupied in spreading and developing its doctrines. [4]

"Disciples"? "Doctrine"? Yes, Huxley saw Darwinian evolution as the new religion. In fact, he coined the word *agnostic* to describe the intellectual position he wanted all thinking individuals to hold with respect to God. Darwin, in later life, used this word in reference to his own religious position. A century later Richard Dawkins could extend the tradition by saying, "Darwin made it possible to be an intellectually fulfilled atheist." [5]

And so another ingredient in the shrink-wrapped concoction is in place: a disdain for theism or belief in God. The final packaging material that had already been created to enclose Darwin's science was ready: one part social theory, one part human genetic determinism, and one part agnosticism mixed with incipient atheism. This sticky substance was spread around the work with such success that to this very day it takes hard work to remove it and expose the essence of the science underneath it.

We need to ask once again if this is a necessary part of the science or if it is only someone's idea of how it should be packaged. When Marty goes into the laboratory, it is only necessary that he use the Darwinian model as a way of developing fruitful research projects with the life systems he is investigating. As an organizing principle, the model works to suggest ways in which viruses, bacteria, human cells—all of life—can be effectively related. The model predicts experimental directions for Marty's work and areas of knowledge for his teaching. There is no point in his day when he must accept the social Darwinism of Spencer, the eugenic ideology of Galton, or the anti-Christian fervor of Huxley in order to make the model work. All of this can be tossed into the trashcan, just like the plastic packaging that surrounded his test tubes and Petri dishes.

In the next chapter we will look at more of the shrink-wrapping of Darwinian science; we will look briefly at sociobiology and evolutionary psychology. These two play a role in our own time that is similar to the role played by social Darwinism, eugenics, and atheism in Darwin's era.

We will then turn back to our map and walk our way up the road, passing creationism in both its biblical and scientific forms, Intelligent Design, and theistic evolution. We will end our journey with a hearty endorsement of our own brand of theistic evolution.

CHAPTER SIX

WHAT DO SOCIOBIOLOGISTS AND EVOLUTIONARY PSYCHOLOGISTS SAY?

Put yourself in the place of a biologist, working in his or her laboratory in the latter part of the 20th century. You have been trained in all of the aspects of the neo-Darwinian model, with its great explanatory and predictive power. In addition, you have accepted that the idea of reductionism, breaking things down into their component parts, works.

In your laboratory you are studying ants. You observe that they have very specific behaviors and that the survival of the ant colony depends on these behaviors. "What if," you ask, "these behaviors are determined by genes? What if these behaviors developed over time by genetic variation and natural selection?"

This is exactly what happened to Harvard entomologist Edward O. Wilson. After working with and charting the behavior of his chosen research subjects, Wilson wrote a book he entitled *Sociobiology: The New Synthesis*. As the phrase *new synthesis* suggests, this modern biologist wanted to add something to the neo-Darwinian synthesis. The secret to understanding social behavior is gene replication—that is, survival of the fittest genes. At the beginning of the book he tells us what his agenda will be:

> In a Darwinian sense the organism does not live for itself. Its primary function is not even to reproduce other organisms; it reproduces genes, and it serves as their temporary carrier. . . . Samuel Butler's famous aphorism, that the chicken is only an egg's way of making another egg, has been modernized: The organism is only DNA's way of making more DNA.[1]

Thus far, the story seems to be just another tale of a research scientist publishing his or her model, built up from observations. If the book had only dealt with the social insects, nothing much more would have been said. However, as the title suggests, Wilson saw his understanding as part of a larger and richer picture of nature. In the second part of the book, he discusses how his model applies at all levels of the biological world. The last chapter is entitled "Man: From Sociobiology to Sociology." It is at this point that the eminent Harvard professor ran into considerable trouble.

Reactions to Wilson's Sociobiological Model

Reaction to the implications of the book were swift, especially within the academic community. Some, of course, vigorously supported the notion that our behavior is governed by our genes. After all, this seems reasonable, given the modern evolutionary model. What's the problem?

31

A number of scholars, among them the late Stephen J. Gould, objected strenuously to this idea. These critics feared the return of social Darwinism and, even worse, the justification of eugenic goals with respect to humans. After all, if our behavior is simply a matter of genetics, then we can, and even should, strive to produce better genomes. Many of the critics still shuddered at the historical echoes of Nazi boots at the doors of those who were to be "ethnically cleansed" in the name of racial improvement. Let us be very clear here. We are not saying that Wilson approved in any way of the horrors of the Holocaust. Quite the opposite is true. However, his critics did not fear his intentions as much as they did the intentions of others who might take up his model and make something ghastly out of it.

The heart of the criticism, however, was the overt reductionism of the agenda, as we can see from the brief quote above. Biologists such as Gould were tiring of what they considered a simplistic view and wanted a more holistic or organic approach to evolutionary theory—an approach that was, in fact, truer to the original spirit of Darwin.

And so a controversy erupted, this time within the hallowed halls of academia itself. Wilson was shouted down by his critics, sometimes in not-so-gentle ways, as when students greeted his appearance on a stage with water balloons. The book and the model it proposed gained a following nonetheless.

Among the champions that Wilson found was Oxford evolutionary biologist Richard Dawkins, whom we have heard from already. In 1976, one year after the appearance of Wilson's work, Dawkins published an influential book called *The Selfish Gene*. Like Wilson, he tells us right away what his purpose is to be:

> The argument of this book is that we, and all other animals, are machines created by our genes. Like successful Chicago gangsters, our genes have survived, in some cases for millions of years, in a highly competitive world. This entitles us to expect certain qualities in our genes. I shall argue that a predominant quality to be expected in a successful gene is ruthless selfishness. [2]

Dawkins then goes on to tell us how the selfishness of our genes plays out, even to the extent of promoting altruistic social behavior. Altruism is the self-sacrificial behavior that Christians have come to expect as a part of the ideal. How is it that even this kind of human activity is dictated by the gene?

Dawkins maintains that it is our genes that control what we do. Our genes have the imperative to survive to the next generation by reproduction. As a result, our genes will cause us to care about the welfare of others, especially if they are closely related to us. This is because they, too, contain these same genes. Our personal genes could care a fig about our own survival, just as long as copies of them make it through.

In an evolutionary sense, behaviors that promote the reproduction of genes will have a positive selection advantage and, according to the model, will have greater representation in future generations. There is evidence for this in animal studies in a combination of phenomena called *kin selection* and *reciprocal altruism*.

Near Marty's home in Taos, New Mexico, are colonies of prairie dogs, the small rodents that live in vast underground towns throughout the western states, and whose interactions with humans have been stormy. Prairie dogs exhibit a curious behavior.

While members of the colony are feeding, a number of them will act as sentinels. At the first sign of trouble, say, the approach of a predator coyote, the sentinels will sound the alarm, barking out their warning for the others to retreat. This behavior exposes the sentinels to danger, since they have to stand up on their hind legs in order to see far enough to detect the danger. The data from observing this behavior suggest that prairie dogs, and other social animals like them, are more likely to sound the alarm if the animals they are protecting are more closely related to them. According to Dawkins, the genes persuade us to protect those with whom we share the most genes, because it is the fittest DNA sequence or gene, not the individual organism, that is destined to survive. Dawkins would interpret this altruistic behavior as the survival imperative of the genes within these rodents, selected over evolutionary time.

From Sociobiology to Evolutionary Psychology

Dawkins's idea was met with both acclamation and rejection, just as had been the fate of Wilson's sociobiology. However, enough scientists accepted this model that it has become the basis for a new field called *evolutionary psychology*.

The Center for Evolutionary Psychology at UC Santa Barbara is a valuable source for understanding this new discipline. [3] On their Web site, they claim, at the outset, a lofty scientific purpose:

> The goal of research in evolutionary psychology is to discover and understand the design of the human mind. Evolutionary psychology is an *approach* to psychology, in which knowledge and principles from evolutionary biology are put to use in research on the structure of the human mind. It is not an area of study, like vision, reasoning, or social behavior. It is a *way of thinking* about psychology that can be applied to any topic within it. [4]

The principles by which evolutionary psychology operate are summarized very nicely by the program at UC Santa Barbara. [5] There are five principles:

Principle 1. The brain is a physical system. It functions as a computer. Its circuits are designed to generate behavior that is appropriate to your environmental circumstances.

Principle 2. Our neural circuits were designed by natural selection to solve problems that our ancestors faced during our species' evolutionary history.

Principle 3. Consciousness is just the tip of the iceberg; most of what goes on in your mind is hidden from you. As a result, your conscious experience can mislead you into thinking that our circuitry is simpler that it really is. Most problems that you experience as easy to solve are very difficult to solve—they require very complicated neural circuitry.

Principle 4. Different neural circuits are specialized for solving different adaptive problems.

Principle 5. Our modern skulls house a Stone Age mind.

How Is Human Behavior the Product of Our Genes?

Evolutionary psychology proposes that modern-day humans have a brain that is the product of selective forces exerted on our Stone Age ancestors. They argue that we are descendants of those who were subject to the Environment of Evolutionary Adaptedness, or EEA. When did this take place? Well, it's not a specific time, but a range of times that may extend back in our history from 10,000 to 10 million years ago.

The idea is that our ancestors were selected for behavior that would have survival and reproductive advantage for their genes. As a result, modules of our brain contain features that exhibit these behaviors. Evolutionary psychologists use this model to discuss a wide range of human behaviors, including some very controversial ones such as the origin of rape.

Is all of this reasonable? We would be the first to agree that there must be some component of our behavior that is related to the genes that underlie the structure of our nervous system. It would seem foolish to think otherwise, given the wealth of data from experimental work with animal systems. But how much is determined by the genes? How much is determined by choice, what Christians and others like to call free will? What is the relative contribution?

It is clear to us that the Christian perspective is not limited to understanding humans as merely the sum of their genes and the physical structures these genes determine. We see ourselves as so much more than that. Our concept of ourselves as created in the image of God, what theologians call the *imago Dei*, means that we have a wider and, we believe, richer view of anthropology and psychology. The human soul, whatever we think that might be, is not, in the Christian view, only so much neural wiring in the brain.

There are severe critics of evolutionary psychology, including the late Stephen J. Gould and the biologists Stephen and Hilary Rose. The Roses published a book of contributed essays, including one from Gould that goes directly at the assumptions of evolutionary psychology and the concept of the selfish gene. [6] The arguments in this book are not based on religious assumptions but offer a persuasive scientific critique, which we discuss in more detail in *Evolution from Creation to New Creation*.

We offer an additional criticism, a criticism of coherence. If Wilson, Dawkins, and the evolutionary psychologists are correct, then all human activity is simply a product of our evolutionary past, and has no real significance beyond the survival value it conferred on our ancestors. If this includes our ethical and religious inclinations, shouldn't it also include the very activity of science itself? Science should not be exempt from this analysis. For all its awe-inspiring progress, isn't the real importance of science's curiosity about the natural world reducible to the reproductive advantage it confers on the most selfish of our genes? We await a response from our colleagues.

CHAPTER SEVEN

WHAT DO THE CREATIONISTS BELIEVE?

A quick look at Web sites such as www.creationism.org will show that creationist organizations can be found in countries all over the world.[1] A look at the home page for the Institute for Creation Research near San Diego, California, www.icr.org, will show that biblical Christianity is at war with godless atheists who believe in Darwinian evolution.

Creationists come in many sizes and shapes: Old Earth Creationism, Young Earth Creationism, Progressive Creationism, and so forth. Of these, the Young Earth Creationists (YEC) emerge as the school of thought with the greatest influence. For the sake of simplicity, we will explain the teaching of YEC in order to describe the overall position of creationism. We will then turn briefly to biblical creationism and progressive creationism.

Zeal for the Gospel

What puts the gas in the tank and powers the creationist movement is zeal for the gospel of Jesus Christ. What is the gospel? Henry Morris, granddaddy of the Institute for Creation Research, turns his eyes toward Jesus Christ. "The Gospel focuses especially on the person and work of the Lord Jesus Christ, the incarnate Creator (John 1:1-3, 14), who died in our place for the sin of the world (John 1:29)," he writes. "An understanding of faith in His bodily resurrection requires an acknowledgement that only He has conquered death, and, therefore, that He is Lord of all, able and sure to restore the whole creation someday to its primeval perfection."

Please notice here the identification of the Creator with the Savior. Notice also the identification of redemption with the creation prior to the fall. "Thus, the Gospel is based on the good news that Christ Himself is the true Creator of all things and the good news that He, therefore, is King of Kings and Lord of Lords, sovereign of the universe, coming again someday to purge all evil and consummate all His purposes in creation."[2] Theologians refer to this position as "high Christology." Accordingly, Christ is identified with all of creation—that is, God created the world through Christ and redeems it through Christ. Such a "high Christology" can be found in traditional Christianity, in contrast to Liberal Protestantism. The latter typically works with a "low Christology," according to which Jesus is the fulfillment of human potential and the teacher of God's love on earth. Both are noble theological traditions. We simply want to point out that the Young Earth Creationism embraces the classic view.

Creationists find that the impersonal and cold-blooded interpretation of nature that is advertised on the packaging of the Darwinian model contradicts what Christians know about the love and grace of God. The immense problem of suffering and evil receives attention in the creationist rejection of evolutionary history. The waste due to the actions of predators and in the idea of extinction is as revolting to creationists as it was to Darwin. Henry Morris, one of the founders of this movement, writes:

> Evolution is inconsistent with God's nature of love. The supposed fact of evolution is best evidenced by the fossils, which eloquently speak of a harsh world, filled with storm and upheaval, disease and famine, struggle for existence and violent death. The accepted mechanism for inducing evolution is overpopulation and a natural selection through extermination of the weak and unfit. A loving God would surely have been more considerate of His creatures than this.[3]

Curiously, both doubting Darwin and monotheist Morris agree on this point: the God of the Bible simply could not employ a process such as Darwin describes "with all its randomness, wastefulness, and cruelty."[4]

What Do Scientific Creationists Actually Teach?

The creationists say that we can only understand creation as it relates to a loving God who creates a physical world in which divine love becomes manifest. This leads creationists to define their basic ideas. We will try to summarize them here in a list of six teachings. Here's a table that presents this set. We will then explain what each one means.

1. There was a sudden creation of the cosmos, of everything that exists, from nothing by divine action.
2. Mutation and natural selection cannot explain development of all living kinds from a single point of origin.
3. Any changes within the originally created kinds of plants and animals can only take place within fixed limits.
4. There was no common descent; apes and humans have separate ancestry.
5. The Earth's geology is explained by the occurrence of catastrophes, including a worldwide flood.
6. The Earth is young and is less than 10,000 years old.

First, the sudden creation of the cosmos, of everything that exists, from nothing by divine action. The term *creation* can refer quite generally to the monotheistic doctrine that the universe we live in is the product of a divine creative act. Creation has not been around for all eternity nor is it only a product of strictly physical principles. Like orthodox Christians in Roman Catholic, Protestant, and Eastern Orthodox circles virtually everywhere, Young Earth Creationists affirm creation out of nothing, *creatio ex nihilo*— that is, God brings the entire cosmos into existence from nothing that preceded it. Time and space and matter and energy and the laws of nature are all products of God's creative Word, and the created order is a product of God's design and purpose. The creationists are clear that they share this commitment with the entire Western monotheistic tradition that includes Jews and Muslims as well as Christians.

What distinguishes scientific creationism from garden variety contemporary Christian theology is the claim that the "creation was mature from its birth." [5] This is a "no growth" theory of creation. No real changes have taken place. No big bang with subsequent development. What is produced by God's creative word is a world complete with an apparent, not a real, past. God created the world looking older than it is. Young Earth Creationists tend to think the divine creative act occurred within the last 10,000 years, even though progressive creationists are less concerned about the length of time involved.

Second, mutation and natural selection cannot explain development of all living kinds from a single point of origin. This means that microevolution is accepted, while macroevolution is denied. Creationists object to Charles Darwin's principle of natural selection on two levels. First, on the broad level, they object because they see it as a godless naturalistic explanation. It appears to be a deliberate attempt to explain natural processes without reference to God. Therefore, by definition, it is atheism under the guise of science. Second, at the level of research, creationists argue that there is no proof that one species evolves into another. Curiously, once these two claims have been made, creationists go on to accept both natural selection and evolution. How is this possible?

Creationists accept both natural selection and evolution, but they confine them to microevolution, to what happens within a species or a so-called kind. What they reject is macroevolution, the transformation of one species or kind into another.

Third, any changes within the originally created kinds of plants and animals can only take place within fixed limits. Here is how what we just said works. The word *kind* is an important one to creationists. It comes from the Bible, where, in the first creation account, Genesis 1:1–2:4a, God creates creatures and asks them to multiply according to their own "kinds." Creationist interpreters find ten "kinds" in Genesis: (1) grass; (2) herbs; (3) fruit trees; (4) sea monsters; (5) other marine animals; (6) birds; (7) beasts of the earth; (8) cattle; (9) crawling animals; and, finally, (10) the human race. As Henry Morris writes, God intends for each kind to remain within its "own particular structure. . . . One 'kind' could not transform itself into another 'kind.' . . . Many different varieties can emerge within the basic framework of each kind, but at the same time such variations can never extend beyond that framework." [6] If *kind* means "species," then no overlap of species is permitted by God.

One of the chief arguments raised by creationists against evolution from one kind or species to another is the supposed absence of transitional forms, what we popularly call the missing links. If one species gradually gave way to a subsequent species and then died out, one would expect its fossil remains to be a record of the transition. Yet, claim the creationists, no such fossil record of transitional species has been found.

Establishment scientists disagree with this, to be sure, claiming, for instance, that transitional forms such as fossils of reptiles with wings demonstrate evolution from sea creatures to flying creatures. Fossils of such transitional forms are discovered almost daily, rendering this creationist argument void.

Fourth, there was no common descent; apes and humans have separate ancestry. Creationists affirm that the human race was especially created by God, as a distinct kind. They refute the standard Darwinian claim that humanity was a product of natural selection from among a variety of prehuman higher primates. In addition, they argue that the entire human race is descended from a single pair of parents, Adam and Eve.

All races and all ethnicities are united, are one. Creationists fear that social Darwinists could support racial discrimination if they say, for example, that separate races descended from separate species of monkeys. Even if Darwinists on the eve of the 20th century might have held such a view, evolutionary theorists in the 21st century do not appeal to common descent to justify racism. In fact, the most recent anthropological models hold that all of humanity present on the Earth today had a common ancestor, a statement that is ironically in agreement with the stand of the creationists!

We commonly use phrases such as, "I'll be a monkey's uncle." However, contemporary evolutionary theory does not actually contend that monkeys were our uncles. Rather than say that we human beings have descended from apes, the theory posits that both apes and humans descended from a common ancestor. Common descent refers to the position that all life shares a single evolutionary ancestry. Despite this distinction, one Web site sells T-shirts saying, "Am I the only person who did not descend from a monkey?"

Fifth, the Earth's geology is explained by the occurrence of catastrophes, including a worldwide flood. Flood geology is a subdiscipline within creationism that provides an alternative explanation for the fossil record, an alternative to uniformitarianism, which is the idea that fossils were formed at a uniform rate over geologically long time periods. The uniformitarian model, coming from geology as seen by Darwin's contemporary, Charles Lyell, matches rock strata containing fossils with the biological history of the development of new species. Creationist catastrophism, as it is called, ascribes to Noah's flood in Genesis 6–8, dated three to five thousand years before Abraham, the reason we find so many fossils in sedimentary rock.

This flood, creationists say, covered the entire globe. It killed off human beings and animals and plants of all sorts in a one-year natural catastrophe. Sediment piled up on the corpses, preventing immediate decay and preserving their structures.

The fossil record supports catastrophism, say creationists, because preserved remains of all life forms can be found together in the same geological strata. Rather than finding simple life forms in the lower strata with more complex and supposedly newer species in the upper strata, lumped together we find fossils for all plants, animals, and human beings, both extinct and contemporary. For instance, they claim that footprints of both dinosaurs and human beings have been found together in the Paluxy Riverbed near Glen Rose, Texas, indicating that dinosaurs had not become extinct prior to the arrival of *Homo sapiens*. The creationist method is to look at the fossil record and provide an explanation compatible with the biblical flood account. "It is not the facts of geology, but only certain interpretations of those facts, that are at variance with Scripture." [7]

Sixth, the Earth is young and is less than 10,000 years old. The above argument against uniformitarian deep geological time suggests that the earth need not be as old as the scientific community presumes. Young Earth Creationists do not feel that they have to defend a young earth; but they do so anyway.

Why do Young Earth Creationists think the universe in which our Earth is found is young? First, they believe the second law of thermodynamics disproves big bang cosmology. This law of nature states that any system, given enough time, will eventually become totally disordered. Your child's room might seem to obey this law. However, the law only applies to systems that are closed, that is, completely cut off from exchange with any other source of matter or energy. The second law measures disorder as a property called *entropy*. Let's say that you pick up all of the toys and clothes in your child's room on a Friday, before he comes home from school. By the end of the weekend, the condition of the room will likely have become completely disordered. A scientist would say that the amount of entropy in the room has increased.

If the universe began with an explosion, then we would expect, over time, that the universe would become more disordered and then devolve because of this increasing entropy. Therefore, evolution as the development of more order could not occur. As a result, creationists can do without big bang cosmology, thank you very much, thereby permitting the creation of a universe basically as we observe it now.

Scientists answer that the Earth is is a temporary exception to entropy. It is not a closed system and, just like you in your child's room, energy can be channeled to the Earth for the creation of order. The Earth is not right now increasing in entropy; rather, by absorbing the sun's input of energy its chaos is leading to the evolution of new and unpredictable forms of order. This is the physics that underlies the biology. As a response, the creationists simply deny the notion that the earth is an open system that absorbs the sun's energy, and rises through chaos to higher levels of self-organizing order. The creationists feel compelled to deny self-organization in nature. Again, the second law is appealed to by creationists as rendering impossible the conditions necessary for evolution to occur. Entropy means that the once highly ordered creation (pre-fall) is on a one-way street toward increased disorder (fallen).

Third, their confidence in catastrophism and belief in a single worldwide flood provides an alternative explanation for what appear to be ancient geological formations. Such arguments permit, though do not require, a young earth.

Finally, they wish to equate the second law itself with the story of Adam and Eve and the fall. They contend that the existence of entropy (disorder) and its inevitable increase as dictated by the second law are results of sin. Thus, their inclination is to equate thermodynamic chaos with evil that is a part of nature, that is, the evils of predation and extinction, are the direct result of the fall.

In addition to shying away from big bang cosmology and the standard interpretation of the law of entropy applied to the universe, scientific creationists also reject claims for deep time on earth based on radiometric dating. This method uses the presence of certain radioactive forms of atoms that are present in the Earth's structure as a kind of clock. These atoms break down and emit radioactivity according to a particular timetable. The method is used to date the age of the Earth.

Now, creationists contend that all of these methods are not only suspicious, but are actually not valid. For instance, carbon-14 dating methods apply only to samples a few thousand years old and cannot be extrapolated accurately to distant points in the past. Using the ratios of certain radioactive forms of certain elements such as uranium, thorium, potassium, or argon in today's mineral-bearing rocks cannot help, because no experimental knowledge of the original ratios exists. Radiochronologists must rely upon a large set of what creationists see as unprovable assumptions; so these methods cannot be trusted. As John Whitcomb and Henry Morris argue, "Not only is there no way to verify the validity of these assumptions, but inherent in these assumptions are factors that assure that the ages so derived, whether accurate or not, will always range in the millions to billions of years." [8] In short, arguments for deep time based upon radiometric dating are circular and therefore false. The earth is young.

As we summarize the key teachings of YEC, notice a most significant theme. The arguments purport to be scientific arguments. Oh yes, they believe what the Bible teaches. But they do not appeal to the authority of the Bible. Rather, they appeal to what they collect as empirical evidence and rational argument. The burden the creationists take on is to demonstrate the validity of their claims through scientific means. This is why they speak of themselves as scientific creationists rather than biblical creationists.

This leads to a point we wish to reiterate. All combatants in the culture war over evolution have a high opinion of science. No one opposes science. Everyone appeals to science. In the case of the scientific creationists, they argue that it will be science that demonstrates the validity of their belief in God as Creator and Redeemer.

Biblical Creationism's Answers in Genesis

We have just looked at *scientific* creationism, where the burden of the argument rests on science. A close relative is *biblical* creationism, where the burden of argument falls on the authority of the Bible.

Ken Ham's international organization, Answers in Genesis, provides a good example. Take a look at his Web site, www.answersingenesis.org. Everyone works with the same scientific facts, argues Ham. The difference is found in the interpretation of the facts. Ham recommends that we look at the facts through the lens of the Bible. "The fear of the LORD is the beginning of knowledge" (Prov 1:7). By putting on Word-of-God glasses, Christians can read scientific claims that will lead to a more accurate reconstruction of what happened at creation.

Ham finds answers in the book of Genesis, once he commits himself to a literal six-day creation. And those days are only 24 hours long. No day-age theory for him, no idea that a Genesis "day" could actually be millions of years long. Yet, he differs from the Young Earth Creationists discussed above. For Ham, the age of the earth is not the focal issue. "We don't want to be known *primarily* as 'young-Earth-creationists,'" he pines on his Web site. "AiG's main thrust is NOT 'young Earth' as such; our emphasis is on Biblical authority." [9] Believing in a young earth is OK, to be sure; but the grounds for this belief should be biblical authority and not scientific argument.

Progressive Creationism

Definitions sometimes come out of controversy. Such a controversy took place within the American Scientific Affiliation (ASA) as it looked forward to the centennial of the publication of Charles Darwin's *Origin of Species* in 1959. This organization of evangelical scientists wanted to give an honest assessment of the theory of evolution. One book, *Evolution and Christian Thought* published in 1959 by Russell L. Mixter of Wheaton College, stirred up controversy. Mixter thought the geological evidence for an old earth was indisputable, and so was the biological evidence for evolutionary development. Scientists of evangelical persuasion who were thinking this way wanted to avoid embracing theistic evolution. *Theistic evolution* was defined as accepting all the evolution Darwin taught while declaring it to be guided by God. This was a no-no. What could they do?

They decided to carve their own path. This group gave their school of thought the name *progressive creationism.* They hold that "God created many species and after their creation they have varied as the result of mutation and selection so what was once one species has become a number of species, probably as many as are now found in an order or family." [10] This attempt at being in the middle-of-the-road position has drawn fire from both the right and the left sides over subsequent years.

One of the contemporary voices speaking on behalf of progressive creationism on radio and television is Hugh Ross. *Reasons to Believe* is the Ross organization with a Web site at: www.reasons.org. Ross believes that the universe is billions of years old. And he believes that creation is ongoing. It's progressive. As an astronomer, he believes that the scientific evidence proves beyond doubt that this is the case. When science speaks, Christians should listen. With two sources of knowledge—biblical revelation of God and scientific revelation of nature—Ross can construct his progressive creationism as the hypothesis that God has increased the complexity of life on earth by successive creations of new life forms over billions of years while miraculously changing the earth to accommodate the new life.

The elements that distinguish progressive creationists from the scientific creationists are two; namely, an old earth and acceptance of macroevolution or the development of new species over time. What distinguishes this position from the biblical creationism of Ken Ham is the use of science as a theological source, rather than restricting knowledge to what the book of Genesis says. In summary, we note that considerable variety exists within the overarching camp of people we know as creationists.

Jehovah's Witnesses on Evolution

The Jehovah's Witnesses belong roughly in the same camp with the biblical creationists, for whom what the Bible says is important. However, their opposition to the Darwinian model is not strictly biblical. It also includes the kind of arguments we find raised by scientific creationists and Intelligent Designers. The evolutionists have failed to make a convincing scientific case, they say. The fossil evidence is too weak to support the evolutionary model; and evolutionary arguments for common descent between humans and apes do not convince them. The gradualism of the Darwinian model cannot explain leaps in complexity, they say, for example, the systemically complex design of the eye, complete with its purpose of seeing. So, for them, Darwinism fails as a science.

Already in the 1960s the Jehovah's Witnesses could blame social Darwinism for corrupting social morals; and they could blame materialism for undermining faith in God.

> Evolution teaching must take its share of the blame for the progressive worsening of crime, delinquency, immorality, and even war. . . . Following the general acceptance of the evolutionary theory, a far more reckless age of violence developed, to which history clearly testifies. We have had two horrible world wars and now we have the threat of a third one. . . . Evolution has thus paved the way for an increase in agnosticism and atheism. [11]

We find a distinctive contribution of the Witnesses most interesting, and relevant to our own position. The Witnesses add a strong sense of the end time, what theologians call *eschatology*, in which the new creation will redefine the present creation. They cannot accept the Darwinian struggle for survival of the fittest as definitive of God's providential plan because the Bible promises a new creation to transform the present creation. They lift up the visions of Hosea 2:18 and Isaiah 11:6-9, where peace is established between the human race and the beasts of the wilderness, and where all creatures live in harmony. This will constitute the healing of nature. "God will greatly bless mankind by eliminating the great unhappiness and suffering caused by poor health, cancer, heart trouble and other diseases." [12]

What is of value here theologically is this: A biblical understanding of God's purpose for the creation must include the promise of new creation, or it fails to apprehend accurately the biblical witness. No amount of haggling over the Genesis picture of the first seven days versus the deep time gradualism of Darwinian evolutionary theory even begins to address the significant theological issue; namely that God's purpose for creation can be discerned only as we look at God's promise for a new creation. The Jehovah's Witnesses get this part of the story right, in our judgment.

What's the Problem with Scientific Creationism?

The problem with the scientific creationists, from our point of view, is not that they are valiant warriors defending the gospel of Jesus Christ. We affirm that very same gospel. Nor is the problem that they revere what the Bible says. We too base our faith on the witness of Holy Scripture. Nor is the problem that they raise scientific arguments to make the case for their alternative theory for the origin and development of life forms. We too respect solid scientific argumentation. We actually like our creationist colleagues. Yet, we have a problem with this position.

Our problem with creationism is that it makes false assumptions regarding how to interpret Scripture; and it fails to provide adequate and testable scientific arguments to make its case. Regarding the method for interpreting Scripture, the creationists derive their approach to Scripture from the history of American fundamentalism. We have a different approach. Our understanding includes recognition of the historical context within which biblical texts were originally composed. We try to contrast the relationship between the original biblical context and our own context, being aware of the drastic change in scientific worldview that has taken place. After all, when the books

> Creationism makes false assumptions regarding how to interpret Scripture, and it fails to provide adequate, testable, and falsifiable scientific arguments.

of the Old Testament were written, the people of the area now called the Middle East thought that the Earth was a flat island of land sitting atop pillars in the primeval ocean, with waters above and waters below, to paraphrase Genesis 1:7. Genesis was written in that scientific context, not ours.

When we interpret the Bible, especially Genesis, we try to match the relationship of text to context. We try to match the biblical text and its original ancient context with our own interpretation of the same biblical text within our modern scientific context. In sum, we try to interpret the theological commitment of the Bible in light of our scientific framework. We don't try to import the science of the ancient Middle East into our theological deliberations.

Although the debate over how to interpret the Bible is important, still more decisive for the controversy is the quality of the scientific arguments the scientific creationists raise. Arguments based on the fossil record sound exciting at first blush, but a closer look shows they are underinvestigated. Geological thrusting explains what creationists count as counterevidence to deep time. Arguments based on the alleged absence of transitional forms from one species to another are almost daily refuted by new paleontological discoveries. For instance, biologist Ken Miller, in his book *Finding Darwin's God*, cites several examples of recent fossil discoveries that show precisely what one would expect from the Darwinian model. [13] Finally, arguments that are based on a denial of common descent are immediately made nonsensical by new knowledge about the continuity of DNA between human beings and all other forms of life, especially the primates. Less than 2 percent of our human genome distinguishes us from chimpanzees.

Perhaps the biggest problem with scientific creationism, from our point of view, is that it is so tragically unnecessary. It adds nothing to the Christian faith; and it risks embarrassing the Christian faith in the public square. By trying to secure the rational credibility of the Christian gospel by arguing over the details of our origins, creationists (with the exception of the Jehovah's Witnesses) virtually overlook one of the most comforting elements in the Christian message, namely, God has promised a destiny for creation in which the redemptive purpose and power of new creation takes precedence.

CHAPTER EIGHT

Is Creationism Just Fundamentalism?

Are creationism and fundamentalism the same thing? No. That is the simple answer. What is fundamental to fundamentalism is appeal to the authority of a divinely inspired and inerrant biblical text. During the fundamentalist-modernist controversy of the 1920s, the authority of the Bible in matters of nature and history was at stake; and fundamentalists defended biblical authority in the face of what they considered to be threats from liberal Christianity. Liberal Protestants in the late 19th century had taken over what is called *higher criticism* of the Bible from German and British scholarship. This was intolerable to what would become the American fundamentalist reaction. Central to fundamentalism is biblical authority based upon inerrant inspiration. If this is the criterion by which we measure, then contemporary Scientific Creationism is not fundamentalism. With some exceptions as we have seen, creationism appeals not to the authority of the Bible but to scientific evidence to justify its claims.

So, no is the simple answer. However, this needs to be qualified. When you open up the Web site at www.creationism.org, the first thing you notice are Bible passages, references to the creation account in Genesis. Why?

Some historical continuity exists between the fundamentalists of the early 20th century and the creationists of the early 21st century. Today's creationists look back to that earlier era and claim fundamentalism's heroes, such as William Jennings Bryan, as their own. Creationists also hold the Bible in high esteem. Even though their focus is on what science reveals, they are confident that science, when properly pursued, will confirm what the Bible says. It is safe to say that biblical fundamentalism and scientific creationism are siblings, but not identical twins.

At the Institute for Creation Research, Henry Morris and John Morris and others customarily distinguish between *biblical creationism* and *scientific creationism*. The former appeals directly to what the Bible says; and it treats Scripture as authoritative. The latter appeals to science first, and this in turn supports what the Bible says. Giving science a certain level of authority to judge scriptural claims and, at least in principle, to risk possible falsification is what earns the label "scientific" in "scientific creationism."

Let us look in a bit more detail at the theology of fundamentalism. Is fundamentalism antiscience? Is fundamentalism antievolution? The answers are no and no. Perhaps today's fundamentalists don't know this about their own beliefs, yet what we say here is still true.

A historical fact well worth noting goes frequently unobserved, namely, the doctrine of creation did not appear on the original list of the Five Fundamentals. The movement we have come to know as *fundamentalism* takes its name from the Five Fundamentals adopted by the General Assembly of the Presbyterian Church in 1910, reaffirmed in 1916 and 1923. These were widely discussed in a series of twelve booklets called *The Fundamentals* published during this period. Fundamental to defining the Christian faith are belief in:

- inerrancy of the Scriptures in their original documents
- deity of Jesus Christ, including virgin birth
- substitutionary atonement
- physical resurrection of Christ
- miracle-working power of Jesus Christ

The above five were approved. Items of theological importance nominated but not voted for inclusion were such things as John Calvin's view on natural depravity, Martin Luther's view on justification by faith alone, the premillenialist promise of a bodily return of Christ, and literal existence of heaven and hell. These four were held in high regard, simply not approved for the list of fundamentals.

Now, here is the point that is so relevant to our present controversy. Conspicuously absent from either the approved list or the secondary list is the doctrine of creation, let alone an antievolutionist interpretation of creation. Science was not at issue. Darwinian evolution was not at issue. In fact, during this period, numerous orthodox theologians close to fundamentalism had incorporated Darwinian evolution into their respective theological belief systems. Stubborn resistance would not accurately describe the mood of the era. A. C. Dixon, the first editor of *The Fundamentals*, felt "a repugnance to the idea that an ape or an orang-utang was my ancestor"; nevertheless, he added that he was willing "to accept the humiliating fact, if proved." [1] He had sufficient respect for science that, if proved, he would change his mind.

"Creation was not even listed as one of the 'five fundamentals' of the faith" sighed Henry Morris. "Several of the *Fundamentalist* booklets were actually written by men who were theistic evolutionists." [2] What we need to conclude here is that theological fundamentalism did not necessarily entail antievolutionism, because creation was not seen to be fundamental to the same degree that redemption and biblical inerrancy were. The startling fact of history is that some fundamentalists were able to reconcile their theology with evolutionary theory.

We are trying here to dispel two popular distortions. First, today's creationism cannot be reduced to yesterday's fundamentalism. Second, even yesterday's fundamentalism was not totally opposed to evolution. So, although most creationists are comfortable thinking of themselves as fundamentalists, the two belief systems are not identical.

> **The startling fact of history is that some fundamentalists were able to reconcile their theology with evolutionary theory.**

Not every fundamentalist is an antievolutionist. Not every antievolutionist is a creationist. Yet every creationist is an antievolutionist.

CHAPTER NINE

WHAT DOES INTELLIGENT DESIGN TEACH?

Ask anyone you see on the street. Is there design in nature? "Of course," they will say, "it's obvious."

It was obvious to Darwin also. Like any one of us, he was impressed with the design that he saw in the living world around him. And he was curious. So he looked for an explanation for that design. The result: descent with modification from a common ancestor through the force of natural selection.

Darwin came up with what we call a "naturalistic" explanation for the design that he saw. In effect, operating as a scientist and using his powers of observation, he proposed a model for how this design would arise in the natural world. Remember that for scientists, especially in the 19th century, the aim became the study of the physical world, and nothing more. Therefore, the explanation—the model—that Darwin came up with had a completely physical basis.

What about This Idea of Intelligent Design? Where Did It Come From?

There are two words that are used in this discussion and they are constantly being confused: *design* and *purpose*. We need to understand what is meant by *design* and how it differs from *purpose*. Things that are designed serve a purpose.

The dictionary definition of *design* includes words such as "pattern" or "plan." We have a sense that it means something that was made, as opposed to something that occurred by chance. By the way, the word *chance* is also misunderstood. What we are talking about is an event in nature that cannot be predicted, something that seems to occur randomly. But, such events are not really random—they actually may obey law-like principles. It's just that they are individually unpredictable.

Let's take an example. Consider, for a moment, the chair you may be sitting on while you read this. It's a simple thing that we all recognize. Sure, you can go out into the forest and sit on a tree stump, but a chair is designed in a special way. We would say that the chair is something that was made or produced.

Now, let's think about who might have made the chair. This person might be the one who actually designed the chair—that is, the person who thought about what was to be made, planned the construction, and perhaps even built the chair. The designer of the chair had a reason for making it, a purpose that the chair is to serve. The simple purpose would be so that you can have something comfortable on which to sit while you read this. We'll leave alone, for now, the other kinds of reasons the designer might have had to make the chair . . . perhaps as a thing of beauty or maybe as a way to make a living.

In the 13th century, St. Thomas Aquinas realized that some things that we observe appear to behave as though there was some purpose behind their behavior. He was using a newly rediscovered descriptive tool—the philosophy of Aristotle—as a way of describing what we see. He took on the job of using this philosophy as a way of describing how a Christian thinks about God.

One of the properties of nature that Aristotle used is the purpose for which a thing is done, what he called the "final cause" of the thing. Aquinas used this property as a way to understand something about God. He said that if you see something in nature that appears to act with purpose, you could conclude that there was an intelligence behind it. His example was an arrow being shot to a target by an archer. Using this analogy, Aquinas said that we might conclude that God governs the universe in the same way that an archer directs an arrow to a target. Notice that he used the word *governs* rather than *designs*.

In spite of Aquinas speaking about governance, people started calling this the "argument from design" in discussions about God. In fact, in the early 19th century, an Anglican cleric and professor named William Paley wrote an entire book of theology arguing that the design we observe in nature is, in fact, "proof" for the existence of God.

The Reverend Paley used the example of coming across a watch on the ground while walking out-of-doors. He argued that you would not assume that it appeared there by accident. You would assume, he concluded, that someone had designed and made the watch. In the same way, he wrote, when we see elements of the natural world as complicated as the human eye, we can only conclude that they were designed by God. Paley's *Natural Theology*, as his book was called, influenced a generation of British students, among them Charles Darwin.

Notice that Paley was talking about the design of the watch, not just the purpose for the watch. Design can be thought of as complicated structure, while purpose is the intention of the one who made that complicated structure. Paley squeezed these two ideas together and, as a result, we have inherited this confusion.

Who Are the Modern-day Proponents of Intelligent Design?

The two most prominent writers about Intelligent Design are a biochemist and a mathematician/philosopher. Michael Behe is a professor of biochemistry at Lehigh University. He wrote the book *Darwin's Black Box*. William Dembski is a professor of science and theology at Southern Seminary who wrote the book called *No Free Lunch*.[1] Both of them argue that the presence of complex designs in the living world cannot be explained by the standard neo-Darwinian model. They say that these designs are "irreducibly complex" or that the designs are "specified," meaning that gradual change by mutation and then natural selection could not have produced them. They both maintain that these types of features can only be explained by the intervention of an Intelligent Designer.

Now, if this were strictly a theological claim there would be no real argument. But the proponents of Intelligent Design argue that this is an equally valid scientific explanation or model and should be taught as an alternative to the Darwinian model. By the way, it isn't that Behe and Dembski reject Darwin's ideas out of hand. On the contrary, they accept the fact that evolutionary theory is a good explanation for much of the data. However, when it comes to these special complex features, they say natural selection does not suffice as an explanation. The presence of a Designer is the only answer.

Is Intelligent Design a Science?

Intelligent Design is being put forward as a scientific model. This means that it must have the properties that we discussed earlier. Remember that a valid scientific model must be both explanatory and predictive. It must be fertile in that it suggests all kinds of experiments that can be done to test the model. It must result in a productive research program that leads to new knowledge about the natural world. Finally, it must ultimately be subject to falsification, if sufficient data warrant this.

How does Intelligent Design stack up? This is really the heart of the problem. We have stated earlier that Intelligent Design is not only bad science; it is not even science at all. Why did we say this?

> Intelligent Design is not only bad science; it is not even science at all.

William Dembski writes impressively about Intelligent Design as a scientific program. He describes an elaborate and mathematically based system by which, he says, any scientist can "detect" what he calls "specified complexity," this special kind of design that he says requires the input of some intelligence. From this detection, he argues, it follows that there must be a transcendent Designer at work. What's wrong with this logic?

Let's go back to that arrow and archer of Aquinas. Remember that science has, as its specific goal, a physical description of the world. It is as though science is able to witness the arrow in flight. Science can study the physical aspects of the arrow; measure its speed and even trajectory. But without being able to "see" that there is an archer and a target, there is no way that science can see any purpose in the flight of the arrow.

Science long ago abandoned the goal of looking for purpose in nature. When our friend Descartes split the world in two—into subjects and objects—he left the purpose part as a function of the mind/spirit/soul domain—that is, purpose belongs to the subjective domain, not the objective. Later on, philosophers such as David Hume decided that science had no business trying to figure out purpose. And so, science set about the work of finding regularities in nature that obeyed physical principles and building models that described these. So it was when Darwin voyaged on the *Beagle* and, upon his return, it became his task to see if the design he observed in the living world could be explained by a strictly physical model.

The Intelligent Design proponents want to argue about who made the arrow, when Aquinas's point was the purpose for which the arrow was fired. We align ourselves with both Aquinas and Darwin and hold that science, by its very structure and agreed upon methods, cannot see a purpose *in* the arrow itself, that is, in nature. We argue instead that a purpose *for* nature can be discerned only when we have the larger picture, when we can see the archer and the intended target. Think of the arrow in flight as everything from the big bang, the cosmic beginning of our universe, to now. That is what science can look at. The Archer and his target are outside of the view of science. That larger picture of nature is something that is studied by philosophers and theologians. Scientists may wish to comment on this from their experience, but they are not using science when they do so.

Robert John Russell, a physicist, ordained minister, and founder of the Center for Theology and the Natural Sciences, gives another way of thinking about Intelligent Design as an alternative scientific model. Russell argues that, if there is indeed a Designer, then he, she, or it can only be one of two possible kinds of things—either a natural agent, that is, a part of the natural world, or a supernatural agent.[2]

So, Russell says, consider the possibility that the Designer is a natural agent. For instance, suppose that the Designer was some sort of extraterrestrial (ET) who came to Earth at the beginning of our history and seeded it with designed living forms. In fact, some Intelligent Design folks have suggested just this scenario. There are two problems with this, Russell argues. First, it must be that this ET designer was so good that he, she, or it left no trace whatsoever on our planet, leaving us to only guess at the work that was done. In this case, we can do nothing with science, since the hypothesis is untestable and unfalsifiable. The second problem is that, if the ET designer is a natural agent, who designed him, her, or it? This produces a logical dilemma called an infinite regression, like images in sets of fun house mirrors where we see ourselves going on forever. This is not a science.

Let's consider then, Russell says, that the Designer is a supernatural agent. This might be God, if you like. In any case, since the agent is, by definition, supernatural, it is again outside of the view of science. We cannot test or falsify this hypothesis using science. As a result, Russell then concludes, whether the Designer is natural or supernatural, Intelligent Design does not belong in the science curriculum. At best, we might find a place for it in the philosophy or theology curriculum. It certainly does not deserve a chapter in a high school biology textbook!

The problem then is that Intelligent Design is not a logical scientific approach. It does not provide a testable or falsifiable hypothesis, any more than creation science does. In the same way that we said the atheistic materialist could not use science to prove that God does not exist, it is also true that the Intelligent Design advocates cannot use their alleged science to prove that God does exist. To be honest, such proof is rarely the stated goal in the writings of Behe and Dembski. But it is the force behind the movement, and a large part of the reason so many are supporting the insertion of this nonscience into the school curriculum.

Teaching the Controversy

Whether or not Intelligent Design offers good science may not matter when it comes to the blinding smoke on the battlefield over evolution in the public school system. The Seattle-based Discovery Institute, which puts up large sums of money to support initiatives, has a strategy. This strategy is called "teaching the controversy."[3] This strategy has two merits. First, by keeping the public discussion stirred up over weaknesses or problems with the Darwinian model, the pressure for Intelligent Design to demonstrate its superior science is relieved. Second, it avoids problems with the U.S.

Constitution's First Amendment, which can be interpreted to prevent religion from being advocated in the public school system. If the strategy would include asking the public schools to teach the doctrines of ID, then secular critics might succeed at complaining that this violates the First Amendment. This is because ID is a religious, not a scientific, position. So, if the Discovery Institute can "teach the controversy" and keep the discussion focused on the alleged weaknesses of the Darwinian model—with each weakness corresponding to an ID proposition—then the ID argument can slip in under the First Amendment radar screen. Showing weaknesses in Darwinism is sufficient reason to warrant studying Intelligent Design as an alternative.

The strategy of "teaching the controversy" is most appealing to the American way of life, because it advocates fairness, balance, open-mindedness. It casts the debate as one of academic freedom, of critical thinking. It shifts our attention away from worries about mixing religion into the public schools. This is a very clever strategy.

ID advocates ask school districts to make available to their students a book, *Of Pandas and People*.[4] This book presents Intelligent Design as an alternative scientific theory holding that various forms of life began abruptly through intelligent agency. This explains the distinctive features already intact for fish with fins and scales, birds with feathers and beaks, and such.

In November 2004 the school district in Dover, Pennsylvania, required that its teachers present a statement to its ninth grade biology students. It said, "Because Darwin's Theory is still a theory, it is still being tested as new evidence is discovered. The theory is not a fact. Gaps in the theory exist for which there is no evidence." The statement followed this description of limitations of the Darwinian model by lifting up Intelligent Design as an alternative. "Intelligent design is an explanation of the origin of life that differs from Darwin's view. The reference book *Of Pandas and People* is available for students to see if they would like to explore this view." A complaint was filed in the U.S. District Court for the Middle District of Pennsylvania against the reading of this statement in high schools on the grounds that "unlike the theory of evolution . . . intelligent design is neither scientific nor a theory in the scientific sense." Rather, "it is an inherently religious argument that falls outside the realm of science."[5] In January 2006, Judge Jones ruled in favor of the complaint against ID. This is an example of "teaching the controversy" that met with controversy by those who do not want a controversy.

In 2005, President George W. Bush had entered the controversy. He sided with Intelligent Design. "Both sides ought to be properly taught," he told reporters.[6]

Why Is Intelligent Design So Attractive?

So what is driving growing support for ID as a part of the science curriculum? Why are so many people susceptible to the Intelligent Design pitch? As we have argued, the basic science of Darwin comes to us shrink-wrapped with a philosophical and social program, neither of which is essential to the model. A membership card as an atheistic materialist is not required to enter the research laboratory. However, these extra wrappings are the parts of the story that repulse the average person, especially those for whom religion is a central and important feature of their lives. To hear scientists such as Richard Dawkins talk about Darwin's model "proving" that the universe is cold, impersonal, and purposeless, and that there is no God is disgusting to them.

Enter the Intelligent Design advocates, with their critiques of the Darwinian model and their offer of an "alternative scientific theory." Their criticisms seem to attack what they call deficiencies within evolutionary science—so-called holes in the fossil record, for instance, which, by the way, are not really holes at all but simply data points waiting to be observed. They are also heard to say that evolution is "just a theory," as though this is a put-down of the science. We have already talked about this objection in connection with our discussion of theories and models in science.

What they are really selling, however, is a way to think about the living world without abandoning the idea of God. We state that throwing out science in the process is not the answer. Science is not the problem—it is that pesky shrink-wrapping again that is the real issue. We've seen how this packaging consists of chunks of atheistic materialism mixed with various pieces of social theory that are blended into the clear plastic covering so many people assume is part of the whole product. At this point we hope you can see through this illusion and have followed us as we have teased away this mess from the science itself. It seems that many of the Intelligent Design proponents have not been able to do this.

In the end, we do not oppose the idea of purpose for nature. After all, both of us are believing Christians who see hope for the world in the loving hands and intentions of the Creator. However, we do not want to have a scientific model that has, as its central position, the idea that some things in living systems are that way just because a Designer intervened into otherwise natural processes to make them that way. If that were the case, then Marty would have no way of teaching our next generation of physicians about how cells work and what goes wrong with them when they form tumors. True, within science, the old paradigm of breaking the cell into pieces that are then summed up is being left behind, in favor of the much richer picture provided by seeing the cell as a network of intricate relationships. Yet, it is still necessary to have a science in which things like networks obey principles that can be investigated, theorized about, tested, and then rejected or refined as necessary. Our future depends on this kind of science. Our relationship as created cocreators, that is, as self-aware beings who participate with God in the work of this world, demands that we use our intelligence to understand the great divine work.

CHAPTER TEN

WHO ARE THE THEISTIC EVOLUTIONISTS, AND WHY ARE THEY SO SILENT?

When it comes to the fireworks going off before school boards, before legislators, and in the courtrooms, it's the Intelligent Design and scientific creationists who are having all the fun. When defenders of establishment science or even atheistic materialism confront their attackers and see who they are, they naturally equate religion with right-wing belligerence. If the only Christians they come in contact with have eyes at the other end of a cultural gun sight, it's easy to think all of Christianity looks like this. Invisible are the theistic evolutionists, those who have made peace between their faith commitments and the Darwinian model of evolution.

The Clergy Letter Project of 2005

In 2005 an e-letter circulated among clergy in North America called the "Clergy Letter Project." Coming in short of a full-fledged theological position, the clergy letter sought with success to collect 10,000 signatures from clergy. It attempted to persuade school boards that the creationists and the ID voices were not the only religious voices. A Bible-based Christianity could still endorse the best science. Here's that e-letter.

An Open Letter Concerning Religion and Science

Within the community of Christian believers there are areas of dispute and disagreement, including the proper way to interpret Holy Scripture. While virtually all Christians take the Bible seriously and hold it to be authoritative in matters of faith and practice, the overwhelming majority do not read the Bible literally, as they would a science textbook. Many of the beloved stories found in the Bible—the Creation, Adam and Eve, Noah and the ark—convey timeless truths about God, human beings, and the proper relationship between Creator and creation expressed in the only form capable of transmitting these truths from generation to generation. Religious truth is of a different order from scientific truth. Its purpose is not to convey scientific information but to transform hearts.

We the undersigned, Christian clergy from many different traditions, believe that the timeless truths of the Bible and the discoveries of modern science may comfortably coexist. We believe that the theory of evolution is a foundational scientific truth, one that has stood up to rigorous scrutiny and upon which much of human knowledge and achievement rests. To reject this truth or to treat it as "one theory among others" is to deliberately embrace scientific ignorance and transmit such ignorance to our children. We believe that among God's good gifts are human minds capable of critical thought and that the failure to fully employ this gift is a rejection of the will of our Creator. To argue that God's loving plan of salvation for humanity precludes the full employment of the God-given faculty of reason is to attempt to limit God, an act of hubris. We urge school board members to preserve the integrity of the science curriculum by affirming the teaching of the theory of evolution as a core component of human knowledge. We ask that science remain science and that religion remain religion, two very different, but complementary, forms of truth.[1]

What we see here is a minimalist position. The letter signers affirm both biblical Christianity and good science. The two coexist. No attempt is made here to integrate the two. In this hot political situation, no need for a full integration is required. All that is required is to make some theological noise to justify teaching our children good science in school. For more sophistication and more silence, one needs to turn to veteran theistic evolutionists.

What Do the Theistic Evolutionists Believe?

The school of thought we are here calling *theistic evolution* is actually a collection of positions that share in common some degree of reconciliation of Christian faith with evolutionary biology. Take a look at our subspectrum for theistic evolution (see below), a graph we described in detail in chapter 6 of *Evolution from Creation to New Creation*. At one end of the subspectrum we find some Christian theologians who reluctantly consent to the truth of evolutionary theory on the grounds that it is scientifically credible. They find themselves almost stuck, so to speak. Because theology is committed to truth, these theologians find themselves obligated to accept evolution whether they like it or not. At the other end of the subspectrum, we find Christian theologians who enthusiastically embrace a developmental and even evolutionary worldview; and these thinkers celebrate the creative and providential directing of God within natural processes.

Those are the two extremes within theistic evolution. Most scholars at work today in the field we know as Science & Religion stand between these two; they reconcile the blind contingencies of random variation and natural selection with divine purpose by offering what we call "a free-will defense" of God as Creator. We will explain.

Danish theologian Niels Henrik Gregersen will provide an example. He argues for the central idea of theistic evolution, namely, God created our world to be self-organizing. God supports nature's self-creativity. God designed nature to be self-creative; and this self-creativity includes us human beings. "*We are living in a world which is so designed that we are enabled to live beyond design.* The world is graciously designed for the freedom of self-development and co-evolution."[2] Regardless of whether scientists can see it or not, the biological world has been created and designed by God to lead to contingency, freedom, and self-organization. We human beings are the products of grace and nature; and we have creative tasks yet ahead of us.

Combining Biblical Inerrancy and Darwinian Evolution

On the minimalist or *truth only* end of the spectrum, we find late 19th-century Princeton theologian, Benjamin Warfield (1851–1921). Warfield was a classical theist

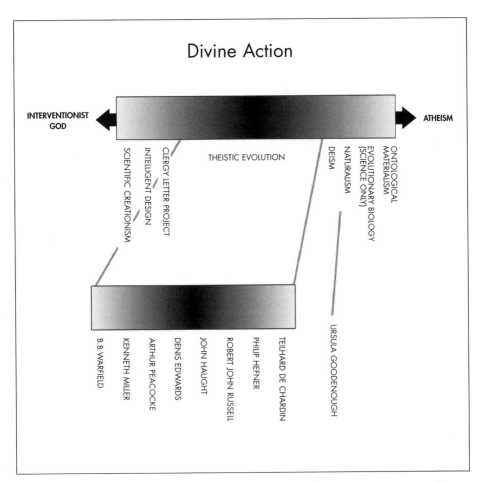

Divine Action

INTERVENTIONIST GOD — ATHEISM

SCIENTIFIC CREATIONISM

INTELLIGENT DESIGN

CLERGY LETTER PROJECT

THEISTIC EVOLUTION

DEISM

NATURALISM

EVOLUTIONARY BIOLOGY (SCIENCE ONLY)

ONTOLOGICAL MATERIALISM

B. B. WARFIELD

KENNETH MILLER

ARTHUR PEACOCKE

DENIS EDWARDS

JOHN HAUGHT

ROBERT JOHN RUSSELL

PHILIP HEFNER

TEILHARD DE CHARDIN

URSULA GOODENOUGH

many would put in the fundamentalist camp. Now, this is very important. It was Warfield's concept of inspiration of the Bible that influenced what became the first of the Five Fundamentals of 1910. In the words of Warfield, "The Scriptures are the joint product of divine and human activities. . . . The whole Bible is recognized as human . . . The whole Bible is recognized as divine."[3] In parallel fashion, the evolutionary history of life is the concurrent (*concursus*) work of both Creator and creatures. That is to say, one of the loudest voices listened to by the early fundamentalists was a Darwinian.

On the other end of the spectrum we place the famous Jesuit paleontologist, Pierre Teilhard de Chardin (1881–1955). Teilhard's task as a theologian-scientist was to take the central Christian message and blend it with evolutionary science. Teilhard retells the story of evolution in terms of a development from inert physical material toward consciousness and then on to spirit. Evolution is the epic that begins with energy and matter and passes through primitive to advanced life forms until thought and finally shared consciousness take us past the original physical beginning. Teilhard held that the creative vibrations give rise to a primitive geochemistry and geotechtonics, and that these same resonances give rise to geobiology. The formation of the earth (geogenesis) promotes the development of life (biogenesis); and biogenesis promotes the development of mind (psychogenesis). We find ourselves now at the stage of *hominisation,* the stage of human awareness or consciousness. We human beings have a *within* as well as a *without.* "Man discovers that *he is nothing else than evolution become conscious of itself.*"[4] At the next stage of evolution, what Teilhard called the *noosphere,* we humans will grow in shared consciousness. Then, once our consciousnesses have merged, we will experience the emergence of a divine center and a cosmic unity.

Teilhard, the theologian-scientist, called this final unity *Point Omega,* after the final letter in the Greek alphabet, omega. "By its structure Omega, in its ultimate principle, can only be a *distinct Centre radiating at the core of a system of centres;* a grouping in which personalization of the All and personalizations of the elements reach their maximum, simultaneously and without merging, under the influence of a supremely autonomous focus of union."[5]

Between the two extremes on our subspectrum we locate a number of scholars, both scientists and theologians, who loosely fit into the category of theistic evolution. Their views are not identical, only similar. They provide the Christian with different models for reconciling if not integrating Christian commitments to an understanding of reality influenced by the Darwinian model. Rather than recite their nuanced and carefully adumbrated views here, we must refer you to a more adequate introduction to each in the larger treatment, *Evolution from Creation to New Creation.*

Creationist Criticisms of Theistic Evolutionists

Theistic evolutionists, quiet as they are, still make enemies. Conservative critics simply don't like this mediating or integrating position.

Ken Ham's *Answers in Genesis* declares that theistic evolutionism is dangerous. Among the dangerous things theistic evolutionists are alleged to claim is this: "in the theistic evolutionary system, God is not the omnipotent Lord of all things."[6] This might apply in some rare cases. However, it does not apply to any of the leading theistic evolutionists we review in *Evolution from Creation to New Creation* or are listed in the middle of our spectrum. Ham simply has it wrong. Quite the contrary, these theistic evolutionists affirm God's omnipotence. They appeal to the free will of God to explain just how an omnipotent Creator could allow or permit self-organization and freedom among creatures. Theistic evolution, according to most proponents, requires divine omnipotence.

Ham further complains that theistic evolutionists deny that "the incarnation of God through His Son Jesus Christ is one of the basic teachings of the Bible."[7] Quite to the contrary, the theistic evolutionists we list on our spectrum (plus Niels Gregersen but with the exception of naturalist Ursula Goodenough) revere the incarnation. This is why many of them give attention to the theology of the cross. The theology of the cross says that in the person of Jesus Christ the eternal God is revealed mysteriously within time, and that finite sufferings—Darwin's waste or Spencer's unfit—are taken up into God's infinite life. What the theistic evolutionists explore is extending what we have learned about God's grace through Jesus Christ to the wider natural world.

56

The majority of Ham's remaining criticisms of theistic evolution have to do with alleged denial of biblical authority. One can understand this, given the position *Answers in Genesis* begins with. What we find the theistic evolutionists struggling with is finding a way to affirm both the faith presented by the ancient Bible and the world-view influenced by modern science. They are committed to the truth of both; and, in slightly different ways, they believe that both can and should be affirmed. The task is not easy. Yet, in our judgment, they pursue it with energy and integrity.

Why the Silence?

Curiously, theistic evolutionists seem to play virtually no role in the public controversy. We hear noise and commotion and protest from the scientific creationists, from ID, and from defensive atheistic materialists, but nary a peep out of the evolutionary theists. *Why?* we wonder.

Let us try on three reasons for size. First, theistic evolutionists do not have a united front. Theistic evolution is a collection of a variety of conscientious attempts to synthesize science with faith. Second, theistic evolutionists do not have wealthy individuals and institutes bankrolling a public promotion program. They're invisible. Third, their respective church communities undervalue their creative contribution. Churches tend to ignore the theistic evolutionists in their midst.

Then again, the problem might be more with the hearing than the speaking. Theistic evolutionists do in fact speak up on occasion. But, alas, nobody finds them interesting. Certainly the media does not. The media prefers to pit one extreme against another in the name of a journalistic fiction, "balance." Commenting on the evolution controversy and the distortions of the media, Paul Krugman wrote an editorial, "Design for Confusion," in the *New York Times*. "Even when reporters do know the difference, the conventions of he-said-she-said journalism get in the way of conveying that knowledge to readers. I once joked that if President Bush said that the Earth was flat, the headlines of news articles would read, 'Opinions Differ on Shape of the Earth.' The headlines on many articles about the intelligent design controversy come pretty close."[8]

We conclude that the conscientious efforts on the part of some of the world's best scientists and best theologians to find a peaceful reconciliation of healthy faith with healthy science are simply too boring for the news. Yet, it could be very valuable for faithful church members and schoolteachers to place books on theistic evolution on their coffee tables at home—perhaps even to read them.

WHAT STAKE DO CHRISTIANS, JEWS, AND MUSLIMS HAVE IN ANTI-DARWINISM?

European theologians visiting the United States frequently remark, "What is this controversy over evolution all about? We don't have anything like this in Europe." It is obvious that the atheism accompanying early Darwinism was from day one threatening to all religion, to be sure. Yet once *Origin of the Species* had been translated into the continental languages, non-English European Christianity adjusted to the scientific core of evolutionary theory quickly. English speakers found it more difficult to adjust. Why?

Today's evolution wars are being fought primarily in North America and other English-speaking parts of the world; and they are being fought primarily with the weapons supplied by American evangelicalism and fundamentalism. Even though frequently the label "Christian" is used, there are many Christians around the world for whom evolution is simply not their issue.

In what follows, we would like to list a number of siblings in the larger Christian family, as well as neighbors in the Jewish and Islamic communities. In each case we will ask: just what stake does this group have in the evolution controversy? Because the conflict with Darwinism takes place primarily in contexts where conservative Protestant Christianity in the form of fundamentalism and evangelicalism is strong, the issues at stake in the conflict are formulated as an expression of the conservative Christian mind-set. It is this tradition that frames the public issues, whether in the words of the scientific creationists or those of Intelligent Design. This framing of the issues just does not interest, let alone grip, the consciences of Roman Catholics, Eastern Orthodox Christians, Liberal Protestants, Jews, or Muslims. In what follows, we will offer advice to each of these traditions that we believe fits its existing theological commitments.

The Mediated vs. Unmediated Bible

Now, we have observed repeatedly that in the evolution wars as they are currently being fought, virtually no war exists between science and religion. This is because everyone on all sides of every battle has a high opinion of science. Everyone promotes good science. Even the scientific creationists and Intelligent Design supporters revere science.

Yet, we would like to observe also that over the last century and a half, concern for how the Bible gets interpreted has generated volatile energy and whipped some in the Christian community into a fighting mood. Why?

Let us try on a hypothesis for size. It goes like this. What is distinctive about the history of the American evangelical and fundamentalist branches on the Christian tree is the tradition of *unmediated* Bible reading. That is, for this tradition, one simply picks up the Bible, reads it, and then proceeds to form patterns for one's daily life, write hymns, construct theology, and comment on government and politics—science too.

If we use the year 1910—the year fundamentalist Christianity was born—as a threshold where American Christians had to make up their minds about how they would read the Bible, we can see the emerging commitment to an unmediated reading of the Bible. After all, said the fundamentalists, the Bible is inspired and inerrant, at least in its now-lost original manuscript. This placed the text of the Bible on a level of authority above all other texts, including scientific texts. This meant that any disagreement would necessarily take the form of one party being right and the other wrong.

Other Christians, in contrast, have been so used to a *mediated* method for reading the Bible that they hardly even think about it. Roman Catholics mediate their interpretation of Scripture through the categories of scholastic philosophy and place the authority to determine the correctness of interpretation in the Vatican's *magisterium*. Eastern Orthodox Christianity allows for multiple levels of biblical interpretation, the lowest level being the literal and the highest the spiritual; and the spiritual interpretation is guided by bishops and tradition. Liberal Protestants have been influenced heavily by German biblical scholarship; and scholarship mediates how the pastor in the pulpit interprets the text on which he or she will preach.

Now, perhaps you the reader are puzzled about the relationship between commitment to science and commitment to the Bible. As we said all along, conservative Christians hold science in high regard. These anti-Darwinists even want to offer a better science. Yet, we have also said that the energy and intensity comes from the unmediated reading of the Bible. How do these two fit together? We need to make one more observation—a historical observation—before we can clear the smoke off the battlefield and see clearly what is going on.

In the 1920s the fundamentalists lost the battle in the courts, because their appeal to the authority of the Bible appeared to the courts and to the wider public to violate the First Amendment prohibition of government preference for one religion over another. The scientific creationists of the 1970s and 1980s saw that such an appeal to religious authority—appeal to the Bible—would be a losing strategy; so they launched an attack against Darwinism on scientific rather than religious grounds. When in the 1980s the courts decided that creationism too is not science, but actually religion in disguise, the battle was lost a second time. By the 1990s Intelligent Design supporters had observed these two previous losing strategies. So the ID strategy has included limiting even more carefully their weapons to a scientific arsenal, trying to prevent a counterattack on religious grounds. The result is that we have religiously motivated science. We are not suggesting that there is anything wrong with religiously motivated science. We simply want to clarify what is going on.

As we turn now to other branches on the Christian tree, and as we ask what stake Jews or Muslims might have in this controversy, we will see how these other traditions contrast with the commitments and strategies of the North American fundamentalists and sympathetic evangelicals.

How Might Roman Catholics Treat Darwinian Evolution?

Roman Catholic theologians, parish priests, nuns, and parochial schoolteachers simply have not confronted the evolution controversy with the same intensity that we find in Evangelical Protestant circles. Yes, in the late 1890s, when the Vatican was taking a stand against modernism in general, there was some doubt regarding the Darwinian model. The Catholic church, like all churches, registered doubt about a view of nature that expunges divine purpose. Yet, this was the same church that inspired the now famous Jesuit paleontologist, Pierre Teilhard de Chardin, to embrace a new vision of creation and redemption based on evolution.[1]

What is decisive is not the creative imagination of a genius such as Teilhard. What is decisive is the role of scholastic philosophy in Roman Catholic thinking. Here we find the distinction between primary and secondary causation. According to this distinction, we attribute the very existence of the world to the ongoing divine act of creation, the primary cause. We attribute to secondary causation the everyday occurrences within the course of contingent world events. The created world exhibits the ability to self-organize, an ability given by God but not directed in detail by God. It is the world of secondary causes that natural scientists study. And whatever the scientists learn is welcome knowledge for Roman Catholics.

It is our judgment that nothing in recent Roman Catholic theology would require any leaning in the direction of anti-Darwinian models of evolution such as Intelligent Design, let alone scientific creationism. Pope John Paul II delivered an elocution to the Pontifical Academy of Sciences in October 1996 in which he said that "evolution is more than a hypothesis." He recognized that this scientific theory is becoming more widely accepted. He granted that "we should speak of *several* theories of evolution," so as to resist endorsing a materialist or reductionist or spiritualist interpretation before engaging in philosophical and theological analysis.[2]

One of your authors here, Marty Hewlett, has enjoyed an entire career as a research biologist while attending Mass regularly and encouraging young Catholics to consider vocations in science. In summary, if you're a Catholic, you have no investment in refuting the Darwinian model on theological grounds.

The main thing we want to advise our Roman Catholic friends is this: be certain to recognize that the Darwinian model of evolution is a model, and only a model. It is not reality, at least not reality in any exhaustive and complete sense. Catholics, like other Christians, need not embrace Darwinism as an ideology, as a materialistic philosophy that denies purpose and denies the existence of God.

How Might Eastern Orthodox Christians Treat the Darwinian Model?

Eastern Orthodox Christians think of themselves as children of a different history. Evolution was born in the West. The Orthodox come from the East. Evolution is not their problem. Yet, these days, many Easterners live in the West. The Greeks, the Armenians, the Carpatho-Russians, the Arab Antiochians, the Eastern Europeans, all have settlements in North America. Conversion to Orthodoxy is taking hold, and the English-speaking Orthodox Church in America is growing. Children from Orthodox families attend the same schools as do Protestants and Catholics along with Jews, Muslims, and secularists. Whether they like it or not, they find themselves involved in the evolution controversy. Which direction will they go? Which direction should they go?

Gayle E. Woloschak is an Orthodox layperson in the Ukrainian tradition. She is also a scientist. She is codirector of the radiation oncology residence program and director of molecular imaging in the Department of Radiology at Northwestern University. She serves on the Social and Moral Issues Commission (SMIC) of the Standing Conference of Canonical Orthodox Bishops of the Americas (SCOBA). Woloschak nearly explodes when she hears of Orthodox persons flirting with creationism or Intelligent Design. She contends emphatically: (1) *creationism is not Orthodox*, because the Orthodox do not employ the kind of literalist interpretation of Scripture common to fundamentalism; (2) *Intelligent Design is not Orthodox*, because its implied proof for the existence of God cannot connect with the Orthodox emphasis on the unfathomable and incomprehensible mystery of God; and (3) *Evolution* could be considered indirectly Orthodox, because Orthodox people are committed to the truth; and the evidence supporting evolutionary theory is so overwhelming that it should be considered true.[3]

Curiously, one ancient, Greek-speaking father of the East, 2nd-century Irenaeus of Lyon, held an evolutionary view. This patristic theologian held that the world was not complete or perfect at the beginning. It would grow. So also would the human race grow. We human beings were created in God's image, he said, relying on Genesis 1:26-29; but we need to grow into God's likeness. We have been created mortal, but we will grow into immortality. Who we are ultimately depends on who we will become.[4] We might think of this as an evolutionary precedent in Christian thinking; but it is not yet formulated in the modern scientific way.

If we human beings evolve, what is decisive for the Orthodox is the evolution from the biological to the spiritual. John D. Zizioulas ascribes a double nature to human beings. We are born into biological existence; and by being baptized into ecclesiological existence we are made ready for eternal life through the resurrection. It is not our biological past but rather our spiritual future that determines who we are. Who we are as God's creatures is not drawn from "what is now but is rooted ontologically in the future, the pledge and earnest of which is the resurrection of Christ."[5] One of the implications is this: regardless of who wins in the dispute over Darwin's model for biological evolution, the Orthodox concern for our future salvation remains untouched. A dispute over the history of biology cannot touch a conviction regarding the future of the resurrection reality.

Also untouched would be the question of deep time when reading the creation account in Genesis 1. Orthodox interpreters of the Bible may simply assume a literal reading of the Bible; yet, they have no investment in limiting the six days of creation to 24-hour days. What is said about time is figurative, and in no way would preclude consonance with the deep time required by evolutionary theory. Vladimir Lossky says that "the six days of Genesis describe for us in a geocentric fashion the unfurling of creation. These six days, which are symbolized by those of the week, are stages less chronological than hierarchical."[6] The sequence of creation in Genesis has symbolic meaning; it is not a chronology of creation events. This implies that a conflict with the biologist's chronology is not likely to arise. What we see in theological leaders such as Zizioulas and Lossky are expositions of the Orthodox faith prior to any confrontation with modern science, or with evolutionary theory.

Let us ask someone on the battlefield how it looks. Keith Frase teaches chemistry and biology in the Olentangy Local School District just north of Columbus in Ohio. He is also an ordained priest in the Orthodox Church in America (OCA), known in this context as Father Stephen. He wants the young adults in his classes to learn the best of science. And something more. He wants them to learn the limits of science. "Science cannot handle metaphysics," he said in personal communication. "Science has its sphere. Faith takes us beyond that sphere into the realm of a broader reality."

When it comes to theological matters, Frase begins by acknowledging mystery. "Just as what happens after we die is a mystery (though a mystery revealed in Christ), so also is creation. None of us were present at the creation of the world. So, none of us can describe exactly what happened. What we can affirm with confidence is that God is responsible for the created order. What we cannot say on theological grounds alone is exactly how."

Fortunately, says the teacher-priest, very little dogma has appeared in history on this topic. Theologians have avoided the temptation of saying more than they can know. "We have the Nicene Creed," he says. "That's just about enough to commit oneself to. It leaves open for discussion some of the details of creation."

Enter the Darwinian model of evolution. It's the standard for contemporary science, therefore, it's what every student should learn. "However, Darwinism is not eternal," he says. "One or two generations down the road, this theory may be replaced by a better one. That's the fate of every scientific theory. It would be a mistake for a theologian to fixate on a theory that could become discredited or obsolete." This means his commitment to the Darwinian model is temporary and very limited, but he sees the importance of students learning about it in order to be well-informed learners.

More needs to be said, however. It would be difficult for an Orthodox Christian to cede to evolutionary theory that nature is devoid of divine purpose or direction. God guides, directs, and participates in the world of creation. Orthodox are theists, not deists. The preeminent participation, of course, is that God enters the created order in the incarnation, in the person of Christ. The Holy Spirit is copresent to physical events. God participates in the world, especially in the day-to-day life of the creatures God loves.

Father Stephen begins with these theological commitments and then interprets his task as a science teacher in light of them. "As an ordained priest of the Orthodox Church in America as well as a certified public science educator in the state of Ohio, I struggle to utilize the best that those who labor in the field of the natural sciences have to offer at this time; and I try as well to avoid compromising 'the faith once for all delivered unto the saints.' This struggle cannot be avoided in the tension over the theory of evolution."

With regard to school board policy, he asks himself, "Will I teach the curriculum as presented to me by my local board of education? Yes. Will I make a point to identify problems with the evidence that supposedly supports evolution? Yes, as is currently permitted by the state of Ohio as well as the board-approved curriculum of my local school district."

Finally, the teacher and priest challenges the members of his churches to stand at attention.

> Now, what do I recommend for the Orthodox Christian who encounters evolutionary teaching? One should take comfort in the fact that the Orthodox Church dogmatizes relatively little compared to some other expressions of Christianity such as Roman Catholicism. On the other hand, every Orthodox Christian must also be aware of the tensions that may exist, such as:
>
> If neo-Darwinian evolution is an accurate description of the development of life on earth, then how does the Orthodox Christian understand death prior to the fall of mankind?
>
> How may the fall have affected life on earth and in the universe? Is evolution a result of the Fall or was it part of the "pre-Fall" environment? Did the fall affect how humanity and the rest of creation experiences the passage of time? Might we agree with Fr. George Florovsky who thought time is eternity fallen?
>
> How do we interpret the teachers of the Church through history who have interpreted the Holy Scriptures literally and allegorically, such as St. Basil, St. John Chrysostom, and St. Ephraim the Syrian, not to mention many others? Do we today emulate their method of interpretation, or do we seek an alternative method?
>
> How does the theory of evolution relate to Orthodox Christian eschatology? Though evolution has as an axiom that species adapt to survive in their changing environments, some such as the Roman Catholic thinker Teilhard de Chardin, extend evolutionary theory to include a spiritual evolution of sorts. How does that relate to the second coming of Christ and the spiritual decay that the apocalyptic scriptures attribute to prior to His return?

Thanks, Father Stephen, for doing our work for us.

How Might Liberal Protestants Treat Darwinism and Anti-Darwinism?

Liberal Protestants are more likely to identify with their Darwinist friends than with the evangelicals and fundamentalists down the block. Just as the fundamentalists see Liberal Protestantism as the enemy, so also do Liberals see the fundamentalists as the enemy. We can expect peace between science and faith long before peace could possibly unite conservative and liberal Christians.

Perhaps the colorful retired Episcopal Bishop of New Jersey, John Shelby Spong, will provide a vivid example of the Liberal Protestant approach. "Darwin shattered biblical literalism and its seven-day creation story," writes Spong iconoclastically. Because the authority of the Bible has been shattered, it follows that contemporary and future Christians can benefit by taking on board the implications of the new science. One such implication is a rewriting of sacred history. There was no Garden of Eden. There was no primal state of perfection. Therefore, we human beings did not fall from anything. "Darwin forced us to acknowledge that there never was a finished and perfect creation. Creation," he asserted, "is an ongoing and unfinished process." What science tells Spong is that there never was something called "the fall."

What does this imply then for Christian understandings of human nature and salvation? It implies that we human beings need to evolve to a higher level of humanity; and it means the saving work of Jesus should be interpreted accordingly. Spong denies that we are fallen sinners; we do not start out innocent and then drop into sin. Rather, we start out sinful and progress to something better. We start out less than human, and we progress toward becoming fully human. With this understanding of the human condition, Spong changes the story of salvation accordingly. Instead of Jesus Christ returning us to a lost innocence, Jesus models what we can become as we evolve further. "To speak of a Christ, who calls and empowers us to be more deeply and fully human, might be the new way to tell that story."[7]

To the extent that we ask Bishop Spong to speak on behalf of the two-century-old tradition of Liberal Protestantism, we can see that Liberals have a double relationship to the Bible. On the one hand, Spong perceives a conflict between the Bible's account of creation and that of Darwin. And he chooses to follow Darwin instead of the Bible. On the other hand, he remains a committed Christian. He seems to be able to reconcile his interpretation of the Bible with its apparent contradiction with the Darwinian parallel. He affirms both Darwin and the Bible. How does he do this? Perhaps this is a question for the good bishop.

Another feature of Bishop Spong's position is worth noting. Not only does he affirm the scientific worldview, he actually calls on the evolutionary process to embellish and buttress the Christian doctrine of salvation. We will evolve toward the kingdom of God, he believes. What he draws from the Darwinian model is a form of progress. Then, he applies this progress to the process of God's saving work and our spiritual goals. Evolution becomes the medium for interpreting salvation.

Spong's optimism regarding evolutionary progress is not shared by all Liberal Protestants. Distinguished Methodist systematic theologian John Cobb, for example, doubts that we have a built-in guarantee that more evolutionary development will lead to more spiritual or moral development. At any moment, he thinks, we could self-destruct. "Many of us can no longer have confidence in an evolutionary future," he writes. When Cobb assesses the environmental crisis and the threat of nuclear war, he concludes, "to destroy ourselves we need only continue in the way we are already going."[8]

What will be our advice to the Liberal Protestants among us? Here it is in four steps. First, stop firing acrimonious invectives against conservative Christians. A defeat of fundamentalism and evangelicalism would add no beautiful blossoms to the liberal branch on the Christian tree. If anything, this bitter rhetoric makes the Christian faith sound ugly to listening secular and non-Christian ears. Second, focus on the scientific core of the Darwinian model of evolution. Avoid the temptation to endorse social Darwinism, sociobiology, evolutionary psychology, or any other ideological shrink-wrapping. Support the Darwinian model for the right reason. The Darwinian model is scientifically fertile; and for this reason it should be taught to our young people in schools. Third, it is important to avoid asking more of evolutionary theory than it can deliver. The Christian understanding of human nature ought not be collapsed into a naïve doctrine of evolutionary progress. John Cobb is right when he alerts us to the fact that every historical moment confronts humanity with a decision to progress or self-destruct. Fourth, consider exploring more thoroughly the options within theistic evolution. But, in exploring theistic evolution, be cautious. Do not ask science to perform the work that theology must. Science is too ephemeral to become constitutive of our religious vision. Allow our basic Christian picture of reality to incorporate the scientific worldview when and where it is complementary.

What Stake Does Judaism Have in the Evolution Controversy?

For most of Judaism, the battle over evolution is somebody else's war. It is not a Jewish problem. The Jewish understanding is that God's creation at the beginning was unfinished; so it is no surprise that a scientific theory such as evolution might arise that shows ongoing creation. In addition, the Hebrew concept of *Tikkun Olam*, according to which we in the human race are mandated by God to fix what is broken in creation, leads to the strong emphasis in Jewish culture on healing, including the scientific pursuit of medicine.

Jewish biblical reading is rich with interpretation. The tradition of *halakhah* permits and even encourages expansion from the tradition-specific character of God's revelation to the chosen people toward universal wisdom and shared knowledge. It permits and even encourages healthy hospitality to science. A conflict with the Darwinian model of evolution is less likely to arise in Judaism than in other religions of the Book.

Medieval theologian Moses Maimonides criticized those who insisted on reading Genesis literally. When the Torah would conflict with what science would say, he would ask that we learn well what science would say. Then, we would modify Torah interpretation accordingly.

By the early 1900s, the majority of Conservative and Reformed Jewish intellectuals had come to accept Darwinism. Some Orthodox Jews down to the present see a conflict between the Darwinian model and allegiance to the biblical account of creation. Some Orthodox Jews find themselves in sympathy with Christian creationists, although the majority of Jews since WWII believe God allows nature and history to run their courses without intervention. In summary, the dominant view of contemporary Judaism is to treat Genesis symbolically or figuratively, not literally; hence, relatively little difficulty with Darwinian evolution has arisen. [9]

We have only one item of advice for our Jewish colleagues: have patience with us Christians.

What Stake Does Islam Have in the Evolution Controversy?

The Islamic religion, like Christianity, was born in an ancient culture now long past; and we all have to mature in a world permeated with modern science. "The global penetration of modern science is a *fait accompli*, whether one likes it or not," writes Muzaffar Iqbal, editor of the journal *Islam and Science*. [10] Some Muslims like it. They believe they can find precursors to modern evolution in their ancient religious roots.

"God is the Creator of everything," says the Qur'an (13:16). Now, did God create once and for all, only at the beginning? Elsewhere we read: "Were we worn out by the first creation?" (50:15). Could this indicate a second creation or, better, continuous creation? Some Muslims such as Mehdi Golshani in Tehran think so. [11] If we find here an opening toward continuing creation, might this include the evolution of species? Might modern science add something that helps us interpret the Qur'an?

Lebanese scholar Husayn al-Jisr (1845–1909), only one generation following Darwin, shows that within Islam we can find honest attempts to reconcile modern science with classic faith. Like Christians worried about the relationship of an authoritative Bible with modern science, Muslims too need to find a way to interpret the Qur'an in light of the new understandings of science. One way is to declare that the new understandings are really not all that new. They were anticipated already in the divinely inspired Qur'an. This was al-Jisr's approach. He would quote passages from the Qur'an such as, "we made every living thing from water," and then argue that this is reconcilable with the Darwinian model of evolution. After all, land animals and birds evolved from water life.

Significant is al-Jisr's self-quiz regarding the origin of species. He could find no evidence within the Qur'an that we must assume all species were fixed at origin. They could have come into existence gradually. He found he could interpret the Qur'an to accommodate the new Darwinian model. [12]

"Today we know that Darwin's theory of evolution is actually the Muslim theory of evolution." [13] These are the words of Muslim scientist T. O. Shanavas, who writes passionately to rescue Muslims tempted to sympathize with Christian creationists and fundamentalists. "Contrary to the current opposition to teaching evolution in American public schools, centuries before Darwin the doctrine of the gradual development of life forms ending in mankind was part of the curriculum in Muslim schools." [14] Premodern Islam could accept such things as deep time and human kinship with the apes; and contemporary Islam celebrates science and encourages the study of science. "Science and religion need not be competing ideologies," he says. [15]

Not every Muslim would concur that we should work this hard to accommodate the tradition to science. The widely respected contemporary Shiite scholar, Seyyed Hossein Nasr, argues that the premodern religious vision has its own integrity. It does not need to be propped up by science. "The religious view of the order of nature must be reasserted on the metaphysical, philosophical, cosmological, and scientific levels as a legitimate knowledge without necessarily denying modern scientific knowledge." [16] Although Nasr respects science, he advises religious persons in general, and Muslims in particular, to remain loyal to the fundamentals of the faith.

With this assumption, Nasr takes a strong stand in opposition to the Darwinian model of evolution, especially the form of atheistic materialism as promulgated by Herbert Spencer and Thomas Huxley. Nasr objects to the exhaustive materialism because the religious vision retains the independent existence of mind, of spirit. The mind is an independent substance, says Nasr. It is a mistake to say that mind simply evolved from a material base. He also finds the expunging of purpose or design absurd, especially when the Darwinists turn right around and embrace the pattern of natural selection. What is this pattern of natural selection if not a design? Darwinism is simply not good science, says Nasr; and it is unnecessarily destructive to religion. "The spread of evolutionism destroyed the very meaning of the sacredness of life and removed from nature any possibility of bearing the imprint of the immutable and the eternal." [17]

Some Muslims go further down the anti-Darwinian road than Nasr. Harun Yahya (the pen name of Adnan Oktar) in Turkey says Darwinism is nonsense. "To believe that all the living things we see on Earth, the flowers with their matchless beauty, fruits, flavors, butterflies, gazelles, rabbits, panthers, birds, and billions of human beings with their different appearances, the cities built by these human beings, the buildings they construct, and bridges all came about by chance from a collection of mud, means taking leave of one's senses." [18] Worse—evolution is satanic. Satan is using the theory of evolution as a deceptive device to woo us away from Allah. Yahya finds alliances with Christian creationists helpful in his battle against Darwinism, especially Darwinism as taught in the Turkish public schools. In Turkey we find virtually an Islamic creationist movement.

In summary, if we place contemporary Islam on our spectrum of perspectives, we could find examples of conservative anti-Darwinism as well as the equivalent of theistic evolution. Whereas Harun Yahya belongs on the creationist end, T. O. Shanavas belongs with the theistic evolutionists. We would place Nasr between them. What we do not find, of course, are examples of ontological materialism or atheism.

What advice do we have for Muslims? We don't want to presume to be speaking with authority, of course. We do not belong to the Islamic tradition. We cannot base what we say on the authority of the Qur'an. What we can offer is only friendly advice, even if unsolicited advice.

Now, we understand that it is frustrating and aggravating for religious communities such as the Islamic community to have to confront a political and educational establishment—such as one finds in Europe, North America, and Turkey—that treats one school of science, Darwinism, as state-supported dogma. The ideological appropriation of natural science by authorities violates the very ethic of science, which should be an open and self-critical enterprise. The temptation in such a case is to see both as the enemy, to see the alliance between secularism and Darwinism as constituting a common enemy to all religion, Islam included. Yet, difficult as it may sound, we recommend distinguishing the two. The Darwinian and neo-Darwinian model of evolution may be worth pursuing even while eschewing atheistic materialism as a secular ideology.

We offer another observation. In pluralistic societies such as North America and Europe, the exclusivity of the Darwinian model in the public schools could count as an advantage for Islam. All religious traditions—Christianity, Judaism, Islam, others—will simultaneously confront the same challenge coming from science. In a situation where Muslims frequently fear marginalization by the established local religion, the exclusive privilege of natural science becomes a form of equalizer.

We do not want to celebrate this too much. What we are recommending here is a small consolation prize. In the best of classroom situations, we would expect a tailormade engagement of the best science with a strong articulation of religious faith so that an integrated picture of the world could grow and provide meaning for our children. Short of this, the most we can request is that the schools provide our children with the best and most up-to-date science. Our religious institutions will have to take over at that point.

	Fundamentalism	Evangelical Protestantism	Liberal Protestantism	Roman Catholicism	Eastern Orthodoxy	Judaism	Islam
Scripture Interpretation	Unmediated	Unmediated	Mediated by Scholarship	Mediated by Tradition	Mediated by Tradition	Mediated by Tradition	Unmediated
Divine Action	Interventionist	Interventionist	Noninterventionist	Interventionist	Interventionist	Noninterventionist	Interventionist
Darwinian Model	Darwinism or Creationism	Darwinism or Intelligent Design	Darwinism or Theistic Evolution	Darwinism or Theistic Evolution	Cautious Darwinism	Darwinism	Creationism or Theistic Evolution

Comparing Religious Views on Darwinism and Anti-Darwinism

We began this chapter by observing that the formulations of the issues in the contemporary evolution wars correspond to the mind-set of conservative North American Protestantism. The conservatives include both the fundamentalists and evangelicals. Although neither group is compelled to reject Darwinism due to internal theological commitments, some still take an anti-Darwinian stance. When fundamentalists turn against the Darwinian model, they tend to identify with creationism. The creationist framework—whether biblical creationism or scientific creationism—fits a literal six-day Genesis account of origins, where God acts once and decisively to create a natural world in which all species are fixed at the beginning.

Both fundamentalists and evangelicals are theists, meaning they believe God acts in nature and history. They hold an interventionist doctrine of divine action. The key divine act for the creationist or the fundamentalist is the first one, the act of creating the world at the beginning. According to Intelligent Design, God also acts in an interventionist way. But the important divine acts occur during the evolution process, not at the beginning. God intervenes in natural processes to elicit jumps in complexity. If evangelical Christians decide to take a turn against Darwinism, they frequently show sympathy to the ID position.

Liberal Protestants shy away from an interventionist understanding of God's action in the material world. Interventionism means God would act in the objective world that science studies. Liberals prefer to see God acting in the subjective world of the human psyche, a place science does not routinely study. God works within the human soul or mind or moral affections. This means a liberal Christian can reconcile science and faith by separating them as Descartes did. A liberal can place Darwinian evolution in the objective world to be studied by science, while placing God's activity in the subjective world of belief that is off-limits to science. Still, some Liberal Protestants will combine God's objective providence with our subjective sense of purpose; the result is the modern doctrine of progress, progress in nature and progress in moral development.

Both Roman Catholic and Eastern Orthodox Christians enjoy traditions of mediated interpretations of Scripture, traditions they inherited from the premodern era. Little or no conflict with modern science seems necessary. When either a Catholic or Orthodox person gets upset over the conflict between evolution's deep time and the short history of Earth implied by the Bible, this could indicate he or she is borrowing a readiness for conflict from a fundamentalist neighbor. It is not surprising to find some of the strongest advocates of theistic evolution coming from within Roman Catholicism. Nor is it surprising to see that to date so little engagement has occurred in Orthodox circles.

Jews, as we've already shown, have a long tradition of mediated interpretation of the Torah, a mediation in which science is a welcome component. The God of biblical Judaism is theistic, creating out of nothing yet shepherding an ongoing creative process. The biblical God is an interventionist God, calling the chosen people into existence and working miracles on occasion. Post-Holocaust Jewish theology tends to see God as noninterventionist. No fear of divine intervention undermines the reliability of nature required by science.

Nearly all Muslims employ an unmediated method of interpretation of the Qur'an that is similar to what we find in conservative Christianity's interpretation of the Bible. Both Muslims and conservative Christians believe in an interventionist God. Some Islamic theologians not mentioned here advocate a theory of occasionalism, according to which God creates the world moment by moment, but each subsequent moment somewhat differently. This permits affirmation of both divine omnipotence as omni-causality—that is, God causes every natural event; nature does not self-organize—as well as constant change. The picture of divine action offered us by Shavanas, howev-er, comes a bit closer to the classical relationship between God as primary cause and natural things ordered according to secondary causes. God gives us freedom, and this freedom results in our functioning causally in a self-organizing natural world. Curiously, we can find within Islam today both theistic evolution and an anti-Darwinism that is allied with Christian creationism.

In summary, to our reading none of these systems of theological thought compel us to reject the Darwinian model for understanding evolutionary biology. They certainly require that we reject ideological overlays such as social Darwinism and ontological materialism. Yet, once we have unwrapped the science from the ideology, science and faith can be found to be at least minimally compatible if not fully integratable.

WHAT CAN WE TEACH OUR CHILDREN IN OUR CHURCHES AND SCHOOLS?

We've already made the point that we believe the experience our young people get in our congregations should encourage them to enjoy what science reveals about nature and to consider a career as a scientist. Science can be a Christian vocation. Our churches should teach this.

What about schools? The position we are taking is this: first, children of every religious tradition, including those from Christian families, should be exposed to the best science.[1] It is the obligation of every school system to provide the highest quality education possible. This means science teachers should be well trained and up-to-date. The ability of today's children to function in tomorrow's world depends on this. No theological reason exists to justify teaching or learning half-baked or inferior science.

Second, it is our position that scientific creationism and Intelligent Design, even if conceived for wholesome reasons by well-intentioned people, do not represent the best science. We measure the quality of science by its fertility. By "fertility" we mean the ability of a scientific theory to generate research projects that lead to new knowledge. What fertility leads to is a progressive research program that advances human understanding of the natural world; and in many cases this advance in understanding leads to innovative technology, such as medical therapy. The theory we know as neo-Darwinian evolution meets this criterion. It's producing new knowledge every day. Scientific medicine, among other fields, benefits from the new knowledge this theory generates. It's the theory that our young people need to know if they are to progress academically in the life sciences and professionally in medical school, nursing, veterinary medicine, or any profession requiring biochemistry. We want to avoid cheating our children by confusing them regarding how we measure successful science.

Third, this implies a full commitment to support the teaching of evolutionary theory and laboratory practice in the public schools, Roman Catholic parochial schools, evangelical Christian day schools, and others. Once this commitment has been made, then consideration can be given to lifting up alternative models. A healthy curriculum will provide room for discussion of the cultural controversy that includes scientific creationism and intelligent design as well as theistic evolution. Because the swirl of controversy whelms all our children on a daily basis, a nonanxious discussion of the spectrum of beliefs should be made available. Once the children return to the laboratory, however, we recommend that the neo-Darwinian model guide what takes place. In sum, we oppose the idea of equal treatment under the label "science" for non-Darwinian models.

Fourth, much more is at stake than simply showing respect for scientific creationism and intelligent design. What is at stake is faith, faith in the God who has created our beautiful world and who promises still more magnificent natural beauty in the future. In a religiously safe setting such as a Roman Catholic parochial school or an evangelical day school, the study of nature should be accompanied by a biblical appreciation for the God of nature. Our faith in God should not be reduced to its bare bones formulation by either the creationists or the Intelligent Design advocates. Our faith is not dependent on either of these theories about evolution. We definitely oppose the misleading association of the Christian faith exclusively with anti-Darwinism. A conscientious teacher should be able to point this out in an inspiring and edifying manner.

Fifth, we affirm that the faith of our biblical ancestors is not out-of-date, nor is it superseded by modern science. The temptation to disqualify religious commitments because they are premodern must be resisted. We agree with evangelical physicist Howard J. van Till, who says, "Presenting the concept of creation as an ancient *religious* belief that has been replaced by a modern *scientific* perspective is entirely unacceptable." [2] Our teachers must avoid embarrassing religion simply because it is old when touting the virtues of the new sciences. Rather, the depth of reality plumbed by faith should be presented as a complement to the surface understandings of the physical world provided by science. Disrespect for religion must be avoided, even in the public school setting.

A Special Word about Roman Catholic Schools

Roman Catholicism has such a rich tradition in the sciences that we want to see this celebrated. For instance, the priest-scientists who played major roles in our understanding of nature should be held up as examples to follow. Figures such as Gregor Mendel and his genetic laws, Georges Lemaitres and big bang cosmology, or Pierre Teilhard de Chardin and paleontology should have their portraits hung in the science laboratories of Catholic high schools. In this way, young students can be encouraged to follow science as a sacred calling that is in no way in conflict with their faith.

With respect to biological evolution itself, it should be taught as the best scientific model that currently explains the observed data, as well as one with predictive value and the possibility for falsification. The Roman Catholic church has spoken about Darwin's theory throughout the 20th century, culminating in the wonderful statements from Pope John Paul II, who wrote in his 1996 message to the Papal Academy of Sciences:

> Today, almost half a century after the publication of [*Humani Generis*], new knowledge leads to the realization that evolution is more than a hypothesis. It is indeed remarkable that this theory has been progressively accepted by researchers, following a series of discoveries in various fields of knowledge. The convergence, neither sought nor fabricated, of the results of work that was conducted independently is in itself a significant argument in favor of this theory. [3]

The attitude in the science classrooms of Roman Catholic schools should exactly follow Pope John Paul II's thoughts that he expressed in a letter to Father George Coyne, head of the Vatican Observatory: "Science can purify religion from error and superstition; religion can purify science from idolatry and false absolutes. Each can draw the other into a wider world, a world in which both can flourish."[4]

CHAPTER THIRTEEN

HOW DO WE CONNECT GOD AND EVOLUTION?

On any given Saturday evening, it's not the scientific creationists or the Intelligent Design advocates who invite us to their home for a barbecue. No. If we have friends, they typically believe in theistic evolution. Although the particular people we have met in life are due to random variation, once natural selection set in we found ourselves hanging out with the theistic evolutionists. This does not mean that we belong to a tightly knit club with a constitution requiring magnetic membership cards, however. We all think for ourselves.

We'd like to share with the reader what we think. The challenge of the Darwinian model of evolution has really made us pause to ponder and deliberate and weigh alternatives. So, what we offer is our best shot. It's something less than final dogma. Yet, we try conscientiously to embody what we recommend, namely, we want to incorporate the best science into the picture of reality painted by our response to the revelation of God in Jesus Christ.

Accepting Darwin

As we said at greater length in *Evolution from Creation to New Creation*, we wish to begin by accepting the Darwinian interpretation of nature. This means an inner *telos* or purpose or design does not stand up and advertise itself in a scientifically observable way. We will not attempt to locate purpose or direction or even value *within nature*. Instead, as Christians, we affirm a divine purpose *for nature*. We plan to look for this divine purpose where it belongs, namely, in God. The purpose for the long history of nature over deep time is not a built-in design or direction. Rather we prophetically contend that this purpose will be revealed eschatologically. Right now, we can only anticipate the future revelation of purpose by looking at the promises of God found in Scriptures. Now, what do we mean by this?

Let's start with an analogy. If you were to pick up a long, straight stick that has fallen from a tree, you might not think of it immediately as possessing an inherent

> We will not attempt to locate purpose or direction or even value *within nature*. Instead, as Christians, we affirm a divine purpose *for nature*.

purpose. If a member of the Masai tribe in Kenya or Tanzania were to happen upon this stick, it might be picked up. Later it might become the shaft of a spear. A young Masai warrior might use it to kill his first lion and establish his manhood. He might even keep the wooden pole for years as a remembrance. The purpose of the fallen stick would not be found in the stick itself; rather, the Masai warrior will have found a purpose for that piece of wood. When it comes to Christian theology, purpose within the created order comes from God.

We don't find purpose at the beginning. Rather, we find it at the end, looking backwards. Purpose comes from what is final looking backward, not from potential lying in wait at the beginning. In fact, the Greek word for end, *telos*, means "end" both as final state and as purpose or goal. God has a telos for nature, even if we can't see it within nature. It is the future act of redemption that determines what previous creation will have meant, and this can be discerned only eschatologically. It is omega that determines alpha.

God's Promised New Creation Provides the Purpose for the Present Creation

We would like to build our picture of a comprehensive and integrated reality on two small biblical cornerstones, namely, Genesis 1:31, "God saw every thing that he had made, and, behold, it was very good" along with Revelation 21:1, "I saw a new heaven and a new earth." Now, we're not absolutely sure how to interpret these, even though we have some good ideas. We're cautious, reminding ourselves of 1 Corinthians 13:12, "now we see through a glass, darkly." Are you ready? Fasten your seat belts for a ride through the history of the cosmos.

We believe that God creates from the future, not the past. God starts with redemption and then draws all of creation toward it. Or, perhaps better said, God's ongoing creative work is also God's redeeming work. Only a redeemed creation will be worthy of the stamp of approval we read in Genesis, "very good."

As we look backward in time, we suggest that the first thing God did for the creation at the moment just prior to the big bang was to give the world a future. God gave the world a future in two senses. The first sense of the future is openness. The gift of a future builds into physical reality its dynamism, openness, contingency, self-organization, and freedom. The future God built into the initial conditions of the big bang included sufficient openness to make possible the evolution from inanimate matter to life and eventually to conscious life. The bestowal of this kind of future is the bestowal to reality of the possibility of becoming something it had never been before. God provided the condition that made and still makes ongoing change possible. And, what God did at the beginning to make the big bang possible is what God is doing every moment, every second. At the very moment you are reading this, God is dispensing to our world a future that is open for variety, for things to organize themselves. God unlocks the present from past causation; and this frees the present for newness in the future. God is unceasing in serving the world in this manner.

By God imparting the quality of openness to the future, God makes room for the distinction between primary and secondary causality. God's direct act is the primary cause. God establishes the world. God gives the world being, and preserves it from falling into nonbeing. God also imparts openness toward a future that can be different from the past. This permits the creaturely world to take action. This permits what we call secondary causation within evolutionary history, leading to unpredictable patterns of self-organization.

The second sense of the future is fulfillment. God gave the world a promise that, in the end, everything would be "very good." God provides the final cause, so to speak, at least in a qualified sense. Anticipating fulfillment, we want to say that future-giving is the way God both creates and redeems the world.

Like a cake in the oven, we and all of reality in the universe are not done yet. We're not ready, but we will be. The world in which we live is still being created. And when it is finally created, it will be redeemed. It'll be ready for a divine feast.

It should be obvious that we do not limit the concept of creation to a single act back at the beginning, back at the big bang or back in Genesis 1. We do not hold a deist view, according to which God creates the world and then goes on vacation to let the world run on its own. Instead, we say that God's creative act of imparting an open future is an ongoing one. We certainly affirm creation from nothing, *creatio ex nihilo*. Yet, we also affirm that the creative power by which God brought being out of nonbeing continues to sustain the world today.

Each moment God imparts openness to the future that releases the present from bondage to past causes. God's creative activity is never ceasing. Each moment the entire physical universe is given its existence in such a way that it is open toward what comes next. This ceaseless future giving by God explains why the laws of nature cannot grip nature in a rigid determinism. It explains why each moment has the freedom to transcend the previous moment. What we see as contingency or chance or self-organization is the result of God's liberating gift of an open future. We call this continuing creation, *creatio continua*.

New Creation as an Emergent Whole

How will we handle perhaps the biggest challenge of the Darwinian model, chance? As we said, we affirm both openness and purpose, but the purpose comes from God's future. It's not built-in. It's imparted.

How do we put this together? We have two thoughts we need to hold together. On the one hand, God's gift of the future to the physical world makes room for evolution by providing openness to change and self-organization. On the other hand, God's long-term future embodies an aim, namely, the harmony and benefit of all God's creatures. In his commentary on Genesis 1:1, Basil of Caesarea says "the world was not created by chance and without reason, but for a useful end and for the great advantage of all beings."[1] Neither alpha nor omega belong to chance, even if much of what happens in between does.

In the meantime, we share a concern with ID, namely, the emergence of complex wholes. We are holists. According to holistic or emergentist thinking, the whole is greater than the sum of the parts. Evolutionary history has witnessed the emergence of living creatures, which as organisms constitute wholes that reorganize and give new meaning to the chemical parts that make them up. No organism can be reduced to its chemical components and retain its identity as a living creature.

We find methodological reductionism OK, but we oppose ontological reductionism. We believe the whole is greater than the sum of the parts, as we just said. A whole cannot be reduced to its parts and remain what it is. Furthermore, new wholes emerge during evolutionary history. We look forward with Teilhard de Chardin to the final whole of wholes, the kingdom of God.

We observe that new wholes transform past parts. Integration into new more comprehensive unities preserve while renewing what came before. This holistic complexification process is nonlinear. Adding a new whole changes an entire situation in a significant way. The degree of transformative effect renders redemption possible. Can we learn something theologically here? By analogy, might we apply what we have observed as emergent holism to God's eschatological promises? Might emergentist thinking cast new light on how we interpret the Bible?

The last book of the Bible, Revelation, promises a new heaven and a new earth. This new reality will transform, yet preserve, the entire history of cosmic creation. What God did at the beginning to draw the physical world from nonbeing into being along with God's continuous sustaining of the natural order during its period of self-organization will be taken up into the consummate new creation. God's creative activity within nature and within human history is derivative from his eschatological act of redeeming the whole of the cosmos. Where we find ourselves today is looking back to alpha, to *creatio ex nihilo*, and looking forward to omega, the new creation *ex vetere*, out of what has come before. The new creation will emerge from what God's Spirit does to the present creation.

We believe the new creation will be a physical creation, even if it is pervaded by the divine Spirit. Think about what passages such as this could mean: "Death will be no more; / mourning and crying and pain will be no more, / for the first things have passed away" (Rev 21:4 NRSV). Is the Bible for real? If it is, then what does this mean? That's what we're trying to picture here.

The violence, suffering, and death so inescapable in Darwin's world will become only a past memory. This is the component of redemption in the new creation. What we have accepted as the laws of nature to date will have to undergo modification. The new creation "can be free from suffering," writes Cambridge theologian and physicist John Polkinghorne, "for it is conceivable that the divinely ordained laws of nature appropriate to a world making itself through its own evolving history should give way to a differently constituted form of 'matter,' appropriate to a universe 'freely returned' from independence to an existence of integration with its Creator."[2] Exactly how the laws of nature could be modified to eliminate the suffering of sentient beings is difficult for our scientifically informed imaginations to conceive, because now we only see through a glass darkly.[3] Yet, nothing short of this is the divine promise. Figuring out how to accomplish it will be up to God's imagination.

From the Theoretical to the Practical

We are doing this theological work because our faith, like so many other people's, is seeking understanding. The task is to interpret the ancient Bible in light of modern science to paint a picture of reality in which all things are oriented toward the God of grace and salvation. Yet, alas, this is at present only our little opinion, although we are not alone in holding these ideas. It's not church dogma. It's one point of view among many in a pluralistic society. But it is an informed point of view, honed by years of study, reflection, and conversation with others from the fields of science and theology. While we are thinking about our eternal God and the history of the cosmos, local schoolteachers are getting subpoenas to appear in court. But we hope our thinking can give you the tools to decipher competing claims and help you unpack the confusing shrink-wrapping around the evolution controversy. Our bottom line is that the best science and our best thinking about God can go together.

CHAPTER FOURTEEN

HOW SHOULD WE INTERPRET THE CREATION STORY IN GENESIS?

The fires of controversy over evolution in our society are fueled in part by the anxiety on the part of Christian believers that the dominate position of the Darwinian model in the public school system will conspire to undermine our faith in a gracious and powerful God. Even more fearsome is that what our children learn in school may influence them for the rest of their life. They could grow up thinking that the natural world is meaningless or pitiless and certainly unbecoming of the God of grace we learn about in our churches. For some families, the fear is that our children will come too close to science and lose their faith. For others, the fear is that our children will be frightened away from science and miss an opportunity for mental excitement and sophisticated service in society.

We in our society attempt to deal with this anxiety in different ways. One way is to turn with a magnifying glass to the texts of the Bible, the inspired Word of God. By poring over verse after verse, we look for clues and signs and mandates and warnings and comfort. We look for God's definitive answer. We look for a map through the wilderness of controversy that will guarantee that we won't get lost. Yet, the anxiety seems only to increase rather than lead us to a peaceful equilibrium.

Here is our antidote to this anxiety. If we are to gain peace of mind, we'll have to answer Jesus' call to faith. We'll have to trust personally in God. "Do not worry about your life," says Jesus in the Sermon on the Mount. "Look at the birds of the air; they neither sow reap nor gather into barns, and yet your heavenly Father feeds them. Are you not of more value than they?" (Matt 6:25-26 NRSV) One thing this can mean is that we need not worry if we fall short of getting it exactly right. We need not worry if our own theoretical view—whether that view is creationism, Intelligent Design, theistic evolution, or what have you—seems solid one day but springs leaks in the theory the next. Our ideas have their own way of evolving as well. Now we see in a glass darkly. Later, St. Paul promises us that we will see God amid the bright light of full truth.

How Should We Read the Book of Genesis?

In the meantime, we need to engage in interpretation of that enigmatic yet magnificent book that opens our Bible, the book of Genesis. How should we go about this?

Our creationist friends want to see Genesis as a record of events that occurred during the first six days of reality a few thousand years ago. Each verse is to be analyzed with literal precision. Within this interpretive filter, they fix their attention on the word *kind*, as we mentioned earlier. In Genesis 1:1–2:4a, God creates creatures and asks them to multiply according to their own "kinds" (Hebrew, *min*). Creationist interpreters identify ten "kinds" in Genesis: (1) grass; (2) herbs; (3) fruit trees; (4) sea monsters; (5) other marine animals; (6) birds; (7) beasts of the earth; (8) cattle; (9) crawling animals; and, finally, (10) the human race. Then, the creationists equate the word *kind* with *species*. Even though the Bible does not use the word *species*, the literal interpretation leads them to this application. Further, it leads them to put up a "no trespassing" sign to prevent species from crossing. The neo-Darwinian model, according to which random variation in genetic mutation combined with environmental influences in natural selection lead to the development of new species from previous species, is judged to be false.

We see three problems with this kind of biblical interpretation. First, it fails to allow for secondary causation. God is the primary cause, according to the creationists; and as the primary cause God creates individual species. What is forbidden is a subsequent history of secondary causation where the world responds to God's command to "bring forth" (Gen 1:20, 24).

We notice something typically unnoticed. In Genesis 1:20 God says "Let the waters bring forth . . ." and in 1:24 God says "Let the earth bring forth . . ." If we were to apply the so-called literal method of interpretation that says *kind* is the equivalent of *species*, we could easily say these verses are the equivalent of God saying "Let the water and the earth bring forth evolution." This would become biblical testimony on behalf of secondary causation.

Second, the creationist interpretation favors a particular point of view. To move from a word such as *kind* to an equation with *species* and then to repudiate libraries of evidence that support the Darwinian model is at minimum tendentious, at maximum intellectually suicidal. It demands a sacrifice of the intellect.

Third, this sort of biblical interpretation makes an assumption that the book of Genesis applies solely to a finished action that happened many years ago. It assumes without question that what God did in the past defines the reality of God's creation. Although it affirms *creatio ex nihilo*, creation from nothing, it implicitly ignores *creatio continua*, continuing creation. It pretends there are no passages in Scripture that describe God doing new things, let alone God's creatures doing new things. Further, it ignores the integral relationship between God's creating and redeeming activity.

What we would like to see considered is interpreting creation in light of new creation. This is what the Protestant Reformers called the "Scripture Principle"—that is, interpreting one passage of Scripture in light of other passages. It is a principle of mediated interpretation.

Here is how it works in our case. Because the God of the Bible is described as doing new things and promising new things (Isa 43:19; Jer 31:22), we would like this mode of newness to influence how we read what Scripture says. So, while looking through a glass darkly yet relying upon the promise God made to us in the Easter resurrection of Jesus (1 Cor 15), we turn our attention to the opening chapter of the book of Genesis.

Can We Read Genesis 1:1–2:4a in Light of Revelation 21:1-4?

As we wrote in our earlier book, *Evolution from Creation to New Creation*, we believe that God's creative work had a beginning. But it did not stop there. God's creative work is ongoing. And it will not be completed until the entire creation is redeemed.

We interpret reality from the perspective of its destiny, from the promised new creation.

What we read in the opening verses of Genesis is how, in the beginning, God began creating by uttering the Word. God's Word is not limited to the beginning, however. God's Word is eternal. Furthermore, that eternal Word is incarnate in Jesus Christ. And we receive God's Word in the form of the Bible's promise. God plans to keep his Word.

With this in mind we ask: might we think of the opening account of creation in Genesis 1:1–2:4a as describing not merely a beginning but also the present time? Could we think of the creation week of seven days as inclusive of the entire history of the creation from big bang to whatever will become of the universe in the future? Could evolutionary history constitute one small episode in the divine epic of creation, "Let the earth bring forth the living creature . . ." (Gen 1:24)? Could we read the beginning of the Bible in light of the end, in light of Revelation 21:1-4 where in the New Jerusalem there will be no more crying nor pain, where tears will be wiped away from eyes, and where death shall be no more?

Could we see ourselves today standing between the initial moment when God opened his divine mouth to say, "Let there be . . ." and the final moment when God declares that, "behold, it is very good"? Could we still be looking forward to the Sabbath day, to God's first day of rest yet in the future?

As you can see, to our reading, this awesome description of God's creative activity is not limited to a completed event back at the beginning. It's inclusive of what's happening now. And it promises Sabbath fulfillment yet in the future.

The Word by which God drew being from nonbeing, drew a physical world out of a nothing that preceded it, is the very same Word by which all of reality is presently sustained and will be consummated. What we are suggesting here is that we consider the future consummation to be the crowning conclusion of God's act of creation. Creation will then turn out to be a single inclusive divine act whereby what comes into existence is perfected in its existence. God will say, as the book of Genesis predicts God will say, "Behold, it is very good," and it will become eternally good. Amen.

NOTES

1. Is There a Battle in Our Classrooms and Congregations?

1. Scott MacKay, "The Evolving Fight Over Darwin," *Providence Journal* (September 29, 2005): A6.

2. See http://news.yahoo.com/s/ap/20051206/ap_on_re_us/creationism_class.

3. We provide a bit more detail on the spectrum in Ted Peters and Martinez Hewlett, *Evolution from Creation to New Creation* (Nashville: Abingdon, 2003), 31, 117.

4. Edward K. Wagner and Martinez J. Hewlett, *Basic Virology* (Oxford: Blackwell, 1999).

5. "A Catechism of Creation: An Episcopal Understanding," http://www.episcopalchurch.org/19021_58393_ENG_HTM.htm?menupage=58392.

6. See our two sessions on evolution at the Web site for the "Thoughtful Christian," www.TheThoughtfulChristian.com.

2. What Did Charles Darwin Actually Say?

1. Charles Darwin, chap. 15, *The Origin of Species by Means of Natural Selection*, 6th ed. (London: 1872).

3. Only a Theory? What Do Research Scientists Actually Do?

1. For more information, see Thomas Kuhns's classic, *The Structure of Scientific Revolutions*, 3rd ed. (Chicago: University of Chicago Press, 1996).

4. Can We Believe in God and Evolution?

1. Francis Crick, *Of Molecules and Men* (Seattle: University of Washington Press, 1966), 10, 14.

2. Richard Dawkins, *River out of Eden* (New York: Basic Books, 1995), 133.

3. Daniel C. Dennett, *Consciousness Explained* (Boston: Little, Brown, and Co., 1991).

4. Richard Lewontin, review of *The Demon-Haunted World: Science as a Candle in the Dark*, by Carl Sagan, *New York Review of Books* (January 9, 1997).

5. Daniel C. Dennett, *Freedom Evolves* (New York: Viking, 2003), 19.

6. Beatrice Bruteau, *God's Ecstasy* (New York: Crossroad Publishing Company, 1997), 10.

7. John Haught, *God after Darwin* (Boulder: Westview Press, 2000), 47.

5. Does Evolution Corrupt Our Values?

1. John D. Morris, foreword to *Kansas Tornado: 1999 Science Curriculum Standards Battle*, by Paul Ackerman and Bob Williams (El Cajon, Calif.: Institute for Creation Research, 1999), 6.

2. Francis Galton, introduction to *Hereditary Genius: An Inquiry into Its Laws and Consequences* (London: McMillan and Company, 1892). The full text is available on the Internet at http://www.mugu.com/galton/. A new biography has recently appeared: Nicholas Wright Gillham, *A Life of Sir Francis Galton* (Oxford and New York: Oxford University Press, 2001).

3. See Huxley's letter at the Web site maintained by Clark University: http://aleph0.clarku.edu/huxley/letters/59.html.

4. Thomas Huxley, "The Coming of Age of the Origin of Species," *Science*, 1:2 (1880): 15-20.

5. Richard Dawkins, *The Blind Watchmaker* (New York and London: W. W. Norton, 1987), 6.

6. What Do Sociobiologists and Evolutionary Psychologists Say?

1. Edward O. Wilson, *Sociobiology: The New Synthesis* (Cambridge: Harvard University Press, 1975).

2. Richard Dawkins, *The Selfish Gene* (Oxford and New York: Oxford University Press, 1976), 2.

3. John Barkow, Leda Cosmides, and John Tooby, *The Adapted Mind* (Oxford University Press, 1995). Leda Cosmides and John Tooby, at the University of California, Santa Barbara, are the two leading figures in this new field. Together with John Barkow, they edited this collection of essays that together have defined this new field.

4. Web address, at the Center for Evolutionary Psychology, University of California, Santa Barbara, is http://www.psych.ucsb.edu/research/cep/primer.html.

5. Ibid.

6. Hilary Rose and Steven Rose, *Alas, Poor Darwin: Arguments Against Evolutionary Psychology* (New York: Harmony Books, 2000).

7. What Do the Creationists Believe?

1. See also Web sites for the Creation Research Society, www.creationresearch.org and Hugh Ross's "Reasons to Believe" ministry, www.reasonstobelieve.org.

2. Henry M. Morris, *History of Modern Creationism,* 2nd ed. (El Cajon, Calif.: Institute for Creation Research, 1993), 297.

3. Henry M. Morris, *Scientific Creationism* (El Cajon, Calif.: Master Books, 1985), 219.

4. Ibid., 228.

5. Ibid., 209. Actually, creationists fall short of unanimity on the complete maturity of the world at the moment of creation, especially the contention that the earth appears to be old when it is believed to be young. See D. Russell Humphreys, *Starlight and Time* (Green Forest, Ark.: Master Books, 1994) and Barry Setterfield, "The Velocity of Light and the Age of the Universe, Part One," *Creation Magazine (Ex Nihilo)* 4:1 (March 1981).

6. Morris, *Scientific Creationism*, 216-17; see Ken Ham, *The Lie: Evolution* (Green Forest, Ark.: Master Books, 1987), 159-60.

7. John C. Whitcomb and Henry M. Morris, *Genesis Flood* (Phillipsburg, N.J.: P&R Publishing, 1961), 118; see chap. V for the fossil argument in flood geology.

8. Ibid., 50.

9. Ken Ham, "A Young Earth—It's Not the Issue!" http://www.answersingenesis.org/docs/1866.asp.

10. Russell L. Mixter cited by Ronald L. Numbers, *The Creationists* (Berkeley: University of California Press, 1991), 181.

11. Watchtower, *Did Man Get Here by Evolution or Creation?* (New York: Watchtower Bible and Tract Society, 1967), 168-70.

12. Ibid., 178.

13. Kenneth Miller, *Finding Darwin's God* (New York: Cliff Street Books, 1999), 264.

8. Is Creationism Just Fundamentalism?

1. A. C. Dixon, cited in Ronald L. Numbers, *The Creationists* (Berkeley: University of California Press, 1991), 38-39.

2. Henry M. Morris, *History of Modern Creationism,* 2nd ed. (El Cajon, Calif.: Institute for Creation Research, 1993), 67-68.

9. What Does Intelligent Design Teach?

1. Michael J. Behe, *Darwin's Black Box* (New York: Simon and Schuster, Touchstone, 1996), and William A. Dembski, *No Free Lunch* (Lanham, Md.: Rowman & Littlefield, 2002).

2. Robert John Russell, "Intelligent Design Is Not Science and Does Not Qualify to Be Taught in Public School Science Classes," *Theology and Science* 3:2 (July 2005): 131-32.

3. Jodi Wilgoren, "Politicized Scholars Put Evolution on the Defensive," *New York Times* (August 21, 2005). http://www.nytimes.com/2005/08/21/national/21evolve.html?ex=1125288000 &en=6fae3.

4. Percival Davis and Dean Kenyon, *Of Pandas and People* (New York: Haughton, 1989).

5. Complaint in the United States District Court for the Middle District of Pennsylvania, December 14, 2004, Tammy Kitzmiller, et al., Plaintiffs; Dover Area School District and Dover Area School District Board of Directors, Defendants.

6. Jamie Schuman, "Schools Should Teach 'Intelligent Design' Theory Alongside Evolution, Bush Says," *The Chronicle of Higher Education* (August 3, 2005). http://chronicle.com/daily/2005/08/2005080303n.htm.

10. Who Are the Theistic Evolutionists, and Why Are They So Silent?

1. "An Open Letter Concerning Religion and Science," http://www.uwosh.edu/colleges/cols/religion_science_collaboration.htm. Reprinted with permission. If you would like to sign this letter, please send an e-mail to mz@uwosh.edu.

2. Niels Henrik Gregersen, "Beyond the Balance: Theology in a Self-Organizing World," in *Design and Disorder*, ed. Niels Henrik Gregersen and Ulf Görman (London and New York: T. & T. Clark, 2002), 79. Gregersen's italics.

3. B. B. Warfield, *Evolution, Science, and Scripture* (Grand Rapids: Baker Books, 2000), 56-57.

4. Pierre Teilhard de Chardin, *The Phenomenon of Man* (New York: Harper, 1959) 220; see also 277.

5. Ibid., 262, italics in original.

6. "10 Dangers of Theistic Evolution," adapted from "The Consequences of Theistic Evolution," in Werner Gitt, *Did God Use Evolution?* http://www.christiananswers.net/q-aig/aig c015.html.

7. Ibid.

8. Paul Krugman, "Design for Confusion," *New York Times* (August 5, 2005), http://www.nytimes.com/2005/08/05/opinion/05krugman.html?th=&emc=th&pagewanted.

11. What Stake Do Christians, Jews, and Muslims Have in Anti-Darwinism?

1. The magnum opus of this most original thinker is *The Phenomenon of Man* (New York: Harper, 1959).

2. *Science and Theology: The New Consonance*, edited by Ted Peters (Boulder: Westview Press, 1998), 150. See also: Robert John Russell, William R. Stoeger, and Francisco J. Ayala, eds., *Evolutionary and Molecular Biology: Scientific Perspectives on Divine Action* (Vatican City State: Vatican Observatory, 1998), which includes the pontiff's essay in the original French as well as the English translation.

3. Gayle E. Woloschak, "Creationism, Intelligent Design, Evolution: An Orthodox Perspective," unpublished paper prepared for Light and Life Publishing Company.

4. Irenaeus, *Against the Heresies*, XXXVIII.3. See Adolph Harnack's commentary in *History of Dogma*, trans. Neil Buchanan, 7 vols. (New York: Dover, 1900, 1961), II:268.

5. John D. Zizioulas, *Being as Communion* (Crestwood, N.Y.: St. Vladimir's Seminary Press, 1993), 64.

6. Vladimir Lossky, *Orthodox Theology: An Introduction* (Crestwood, N.Y.: St. Vladimir's Seminary Press, 1989), 64.

7. *Bishop Spong Q&A* (July 6, 2005), www.johnshelbyspong.com.

8. John B. Cobb, Jr., *Liberal Christianity at the Crossroads* (Louisville, Ky.: Westminster/John Knox Press, 1973), 20-21.

9. See Web site for "Judaism and Evolution," http://en.wikipedia.org/wiki/Jewish_creationism.

10. Muzaffar Iqbal, *Islam and Science* (Aldershot, U.K.: Ashgate, 2002), xvii.

11. Medhi Golshani, "Creation in the Islamic Outlook and in Modern Cosmology," in *God, Life, and the Cosmos: Christian and Islamic Perspectives*, ed. by Ted Peters, Muzaffar Iqbal, and Syed Nomanul Haq (Aldershot, U.K.: Ashgate, 2002), 224.

12. Iqbal, *Islam and Science*, 276.

13. T. O. Shanavas, *Creation and/or Evolution: An Islamic Perspective* (Philadelphia: Xlibris, 2005), 123.

14. Ibid., 124.

15. Ibid., 11.

16. Seyyed Hossein Nasr, *Religion and the Order of Nature* (Oxford and New York: Oxford University Press, 1996), 6.

17. Ibid., 146.

18. Harun Yahya, "The Theory of Evolution: A Unique Deception in the History of the World," See his book *The Evolution Deceit* (Istanbul: Okur Publishing, 2000). http://www.harun yahya.com/articles/unique_deception_evolution.php.

12. What Can We Teach Our Children in Our Churches and Schools?

1. A helpful resource for public school education and a defense of the merits of the Darwinian model is the National Center for Science Education in Oakland, California, directed by a former University of California professor of biochemistry, Eugenie Scott. www.ncseweb.org.

2. Howard J. Van Till, *The Fourth Day* (Grand Rapids: Eerdmans, 1986), 267. Van Till's italics.

3. Pope John Paul II, "Evolution and the Living God," in *Science and Theology: The New Consonance*, ed. Ted Peters (Boulder: Westview Press, 1998), 150.

4. Pope John Paul II, "Message from His Holiness John Paul II," in *Physics, Philosophy, and Theology*, ed. by Robert John Russell, William Stoeger, and George V. Coyne (Notre Dame, Ind.: University of Notre Dame Press), M13.

13. How Do We Connect God and Evolution?

1. Basil the Great, *The Hexaemeron,* Homily I:6.

2. John Polkinghorne, *The Faith of a Physicist* (Princeton, N.J.: Princeton University Press, 1994), 167.

3. Attempting to conceive of eschatological nature is the task of Ted Peters, Robert John Russell, and Michael Welker, eds., *Resurrection: Scientific and Theological Assessments* (Grand Rapids: William B. Eerdmans, 2002).

GLOSSARY

Adaptationism. The concept in evolutionary theory that changes in a population represent adaptations to existing environmental conditions. Such adaptations result from the selection of variants in the population. These variants arise gradually over long periods of time by the random action of natural processes.

Altruism. In common parlance, altruism refers to our motive to seek the welfare of someone else, someone who is other to us. In sociobiology and evolutionary psychology, altruism refers to enhancing another organism's reproductive potential while diminishing one's own reproductive potential. Because the gene is always selfish, those whom the altruist serves will be kin—that is, those who share a large number of genes.

Archonic. From the Greek word arche, meaning both "beginning" and "governance." We find it in compound words such as "hierarchy" or "monarchy" or "archaeological." Archonic thinking presumes that the way something begins determines its being or essence or identity.

Aseity. Independence. God is a free being solely responsible for the divine being. God is not dependent upon anything else. Believed by theists and deists, but not pantheists or panentheists.

Atheism. A doctrine that says God does not exist.

Catastrophism. An explanation for the occurrence of features of the earth as a result of catastrophic events, such as floods or earthquakes. Although discredited with respect to the biblical flood of Noah, catastrophic events such as meteorite or comet impacts are invoked in the case of mass extinction.

Common Descent. The evolutionary principle that all life, including human life, shares a common descent from the beginning and shares a relationship on the evolutionary tree. Humans are not separately created.

Concursus. Cooperation of divine action with the action of finite creatures. Mediate concursus describes God's gift of the capacity of creatures to act contingently or independently; immediate concursus refers to the simultaneous exercise of divine action within human actions. B. B. Warfield applies immediate concursus to the cooperation of the Bible's writers with the inspiration of the Holy Spirit. Some theistic evolutionists apply mediate concursus to natural selection as divine activity in the world.

Contingency. The process by which events take place as a result of chance or random processes. The idea that such events are unpredictable.

Creatio continua. Continuing creation.

Creatio ex nihilo. Creation out of nothing.

Creationism. This term has three meanings. First, at the most abstract, it refers to the deistic or theistic belief that God created the entire natural world, that the natural world is not self-originating. Second, it refers to an ancient Christian belief still advocated by the Vatican that God creates each human soul *de novo*, brand new, either at birth or at conception. Third, it refers to the school of thought that denies Darwinian evolutionary theory by denying that natural selection can explain either the origin of life or the origin of new species. This anti-evolutionary creationism comes in two forms: (a) biblical creationism that relies upon the authority of the Bible, or (b) scientific creationism that relies upon scientific argumentation to establish the necessity for belief in God as creator of the natural world.

Day-age Theory. Theory within conservative biblical interpretation that assigns one thousand years or an indefinite period of time to each of the seven days of creation in Genesis 1:1–2:4a.

Deism. The belief that a God with aseity created from nothing the world complete with its material content and the laws to govern it; then God absented the divine self to permit the world to undergo its own self-guided development. Deists usually deny miracles and other forms of divine intervention into nature's closed causal nexus.

Descent with Modification. The way in which common descent leads to the observed diversity of species. Modifications, in this case, refer to variations in populations that increase the reproductive fitness of individuals.

Determinism. A mechanistic view of the natural world in which events are a predictable result of natural processes.

Divine Action. God acts as primary cause when creating the world de novo, when originating the natural world. God also acts within the created world, which ordinarily operates according to secondary causes or the laws of nature. Such divine action can be interventionist—that is, affecting or contravening the laws of nature—or noninterventionist—that is, in concurrence with the laws of nature.

Emergence. The principle that higher order structures are not explainable as the sum of the parts, but rather emerge from the complexity of the system.

Empiricism. The philosophical position that all knowledge arises from direct experience provided by the physical senses. When applied to the scientific enterprise, it includes the idea that direct experimental investigation is the proper way of gaining knowledge about the natural world.

Environment of Evolutionary Adaptedness (EEA). The environment in evolutionary history wherein a particular species adapted—that is, became reproductively successful.

Epigenesis. Literally, a second genesis. The emergence of new complex physical forms that transcend the constituent elements that make them up. Our use of "epigenesis" comes from Jan Smuts; it is not used here as E. O. Wilson does, where it refers to extra-genetic phenomena such as culture, which are constrained by genetic rules. Epigenesis is a sister concept to emergence and holism.

Epistemology. The branch of philosophy dealing with how one can have knowledge.

Eschatology. The doctrine of last things, which in Christian theology include: death, resurrection, consummation, kingdom of God, new creation, heaven, and hell.

Eugenics. The attempt to improve the human race by interventionist approaches. Positive eugenics involves the encouragement of breeding by certain desired types. Negative eugenics involves the culling of undesired types.

Evolutionary Psychology. The discipline that attempts to understand human behavior as a consequence of genetically determined traits that evolved during a specific period in human history, characterized as the environment of evolutionary adaptedness. Sometimes a synonym for sociobiology.

Explanatory Adequacy. A criterion for testing the relative value of a theory or model by measuring the scope of its power to illuminate data, experience, or other forms of existing knowledge. Applying to both theology and science, a conceptual model is explanatorily adequate if it is (1) applicable to what is known, (2) sufficiently comprehensive that all relevant knowledge is included, (3) logical or consistent, and (4) sufficiently coherent so that various components of the model imply other components and the whole.

Fitness. The relative ability of one species to be reproductively successful compared to another species under a given set of conditions. The larger the number of viable fertile offspring, the more fit.

Free-will Defense. Primarily within the tradition of Christian theism, free will is appealed to for explaining why the natural world operates independently of divine action and why evil in the form of sin, suffering, and death exists. Accordingly, God is free. Out of freedom God decides to restrict the scope of divine power so that creatures can become autonomous in the exercise of creaturely power. This results in human beings having a measure of freedom as well. Creaturely freedom becomes the condition whereby the created order can deviate from the divine will; and free creaturely action introduces evil into God's otherwise good creation. God is thereby defended from the charge of perpetrating evil. Sometimes, evil is considered a price worth paying for creatures to enjoy their God-given freedom.

Fundamentalism. A form of conservative Protestantism originating in America in 1910, which holds tenaciously to the "five fundamentals" of orthodox Christian belief: (1) verbal inspiration and inerrancy of Scripture; (2) deity of Jesus Christ; (3) substitutionary atonement; (4) physical resurrection of Jesus Christ; and (5) miracles. The energy of fundamentalism rises from its vehement opposition to the use of higher criticism in liberal protestantism when interpreting the Bible. Fundamentalism was not originally anti-science, nor anti-Darwinian. Its opposition to evolutionary theory developed as creationism developed.

Gap Theory. A theory within conservative biblical interpretation that places a temporal gap within Genesis 1:1-2 for an unidentified previous creation that was destroyed, accounting for the fossil evidence of ancient life-forms. Genesis 1:2 is translated "the earth became formless and void" rather than "the earth was formless and void." An original creation fell with Satan; so Genesis 1:3ff describes the present but second creation.

Gene, Genetics. The set of principles elucidated by Gregor Mendel that describe the quantitative laws by which traits are passed from one generation to the next. The gene itself can be defined as the unit of inheritance or as a specific set of base sequences in the DNA molecule that is the chemical structure of the genetic information.

Gradualism. The process whereby evolution proceeds by small, incremental changes. In the language of neo-Darwinian theory, gradualism presupposes that the small changes represent single base mutations in DNA, resulting in gradual variations that are subject to natural selection.

Group Selection. The effect of natural selection on a group of individuals not necessarily genetically related to one another.

Holism. The doctrine that the whole is greater than the sum of its parts. "Holism" is typically applied to the emergence of new life-forms, organisms that cannot be reduced to the chemical parts that make them up. A sister concept to emergence and epigenesis; the opposite of reductionism.

Human Evil. Sin, or the suffering caused by sin.

Imago Dei. "In the image of God," a reference to the statement of the creation of humankind as found in Genesis 1:26.

Intelligent Design. The theory that the observation of design in the natural world is an indicator of the action of an intelligence. Design, in this case, is defined as a kind of complexity that cannot be explained by appealing to natural processes (see Irreducible Complexity).

Interventionist Divine Action. Refers to God's action within the created world that affects or even contravenes the existing nexus of secondary causation. Miracles would be a traditional example. Leaps in evolutionary advance caused by Intelligent Design would be a contemporary example.

Irreducible Complexity. A single system composed of several interacting parts that contribute to the basic function, in which the removal of any one of the parts cripples the system. According to Intelligent Design advocates, such a structure is said to be irreducibly complex if one assumes that the structure could not have originated by natural processes, especially by gradualistic processes (see Gradualism).

Kin Preference. A correlate doctrine to the selfish gene within sociobiology, asserting that an organism will protect those who are genetically close to it in order to employ social organization in the service of perpetuating its own genetic code. Reciprocal altruism or mutual support usually engages other organisms that are genetically proximate—that is, kin. Xenophobia or fear of strangers applies to non-kin organisms that are genetically distant and hence not worth protecting until the age of reproduction.

Kind. The term "kind" as found in the first chapter of Genesis is employed by creationists as a near equivalent to "species." Creationists believe evolutionary change can occur within a kind (microevolution); but they oppose the contention that one kind can evolve into another kind (macroevolution). God fixed the kinds at creation (see Preformitarianism).

Logical Positivism. The philosophical position that science proceeds by the application of empirical methods and by the verification of theories.

Macroevolution. Natural selection applied to change as one species gives way to a subsequent species (see Speciation).

Materialism, Ontological Materialism. A form of naturalism that explicitly holds that the physical world of nature is self-explanatory, self-originating, and self-sufficient. Ontological materialism is usually associated with secular humanism and atheism.

Metaphysics. Literally, the philosophy beyond physics. In classical philosophy going back to Aristotle, metaphysics is the conceptual study of being qua being (see Ontology), utilizing the most comprehensive and inclusive descriptions of reality as a whole and the relations of its various parts. In the hermetic tradition and contemporary new age spirituality, "metaphysics" refers to supra-sensible or mystical realities. In this book, we use "metaphysics" in the classical philosophical sense.

Microevolution. Natural selection applied to change within a species.

Model. Conceptual models are produced in science when observations and data are incorporated into a testable structure that attempts to explain the observations and data. Models serve to approximate, to some extent, the real world situation.

Natural Evil, Physical Evil. Suffering caused to either human or nonhuman entities by natural forces other than sin. Disease, earthquakes, and bad weather are frequently described as natural evils because of the suffering they cause.

Natural Selection. The driving force of Darwinian evolution. Natural selection operates when a set of conditions differentiates between two variants in a population, based on their ability to reproduce successfully. As a result, the variant that can reproduce more successfully (or, is most fit) tends to be more represented in subsequent generations.

Natural Theology. An attempt to discern spiritual presence in nature or to arrive at proof for the existence of God through an appreciation of design and purpose in nature. In contrast to Theology of Nature, which relies on special revelation, Natural Theology relies on general revelation—that is, it presumes that God reveals divine presence within the natural realm in addition to any revelation that might take place in history or Scripture.

Naturalism. A philosophical position that presumes nature is self-sufficient and self-explanatory and the basis for human social and ethical values. Naturalism denies divine transcendence. In the context of the evolution controversy, naturalism provides the core commitments for ontological materialism, secular humanism, sociobiology, and related positions.

Naturalistic Fallacy. The logical fallacy of arguing that a moral *ought* can be based on the observation of what *is* the case in nature. Most often the fallacy is committed by evolutionary naturalists who want to provide a social ethic based upon what they observe in the nonhuman natural world. Some sociobiologists such as E. O. Wilson claim their ethical *ought* can be grounded in nature's *is* without committing a logical fallacy.

Noninterventionist Divine Action. God's action within the created world of natural processes without contravening or replacing secondary causation. Divine action at the level of quantum contingency as proposed by Robert John Russell would be an example of noninterventionist divine action. This contrasts with interventionist divine action, as we find it in miracles, and with the absence of divine action, as we find it described by deism.

Ontology. The philosophy of being.

Panentheism. Belief that the being of the world is in God and the being of God is in the world; but the world does not exhaust the being of God. God here has no aseity; rather, God is as dependent on nature as nature is dependent on God. Panentheism can be found among contemporary Whiteheadian process theologians and eco-feminists.

Pantheism. Literally the belief that all is divine, that the being of the divine is present within all living things and, in some cases, all physical things. The material world and God are coextensive. Pantheism can be found among American transcendentalists, Hindus, and new age spirituality.

Paradigm, Paradigm Shift. As defined by the philosopher and historian of science, Thomas Kuhn, a paradigm is a part of the underlying assumptions or working models in a discipline. When such paradigms no longer serve to elucidate problems in a discipline, they may be changed or altered. Kuhn argued that such paradigm shifts are how science progresses.

Preformitarianism. The pre-Darwinian idea that all of the observed diversity in nature had been created as it currently exists. Common to Artisotle and scientific creationism.

Primary Cause. In Aristotelian and Thomistic thought, a cause that has no prior cause (uncaused cause). God's action is the primary cause of creation, in complementary contrast to secondary causes operative within creation.

Providence. Divine care for—providing for—creatures through guidance of natural processes and events.

Punctuated Equilibrium. An evolutionary model proposed by Stephen J. Gould, Richard Lowentin, and others to explain gaps in the fossil record. According to this model, species are stable for long periods of time and then go through short (in geological terms) periods of rapid variation.

Reciprocal Altruism. Reciprocity ordinarily means mutual exchange. In sociobiology, reciprocal altruism is the service of an organism to enhance the reproductive fitness of another organism or of a community of organisms with shared genes.

Reductionism. The attempt to explain one level of organization by the principles at work at a lower level of organization. For instance, the attempt to explain all biology using the principles of chemistry and physics. When used as a protocol for experimental investigation, reductionism is a method. However, when taken as a theory of knowledge (epistemology) or a theory of being (ontology), reductionism is then a philosophical position.

Reproductive Fitness. The likelihood that one variant in a population will be more likely to reproduce and pass on its traits to the next generation, under a given set of circumstances.

Saltation. A sudden or abrupt change that brings about a new form of a thing.

Secondary Cause. In Aristotelian and Thomistic thought, a thing or event that proceeds from a prior cause. All secondary causes are the result of prior secondary causes or of the primary cause.

Selfish Gene. A term coined by Richard Dawkins, now common to sociobiology, referring to the inherent propensity of DNA nucleotide sequences to seek replication through reproduction of organisms.

Social Darwinism. Deriving from Herbert Spencer, various forms of social Darwinism employ natural selection, including reproductive fitness, to analyze human social behavior with moral approval of such principles as survival of the fittest.

Sociobiology. The study of social behavior in animals with implications for human social behavior based upon assumptions regarding genetic replication. E. O. Wilson and Richard Dawkins are considered leaders in sociobiology.

Speciation. The statement that new species arise by natural selection from preexisting species. Gradualism predicts that speciation occurred over a long period of time by slow changes. Punctuated equilibrium predicts that species arose during periods of increased variation, but that species were stable in between such periods.

Species. A distinct class of organisms or kind that share common characteristics. Members of a species can breed successfully within their species but not outside their species. The one word "species" is both singular and plural.

Survival of the Fittest. Although scientifically this refers to reproductive fitness in natural selection, sometimes it drifts toward a general moral approval of the strong eliminating the weak in society. Coined by Herbert Spencer and adopted by Charles Darwin as a synonym for natural selection.

Teleology. Theory of purpose.

Teleonomy. The appearance of design or purpose in natural functions that can actually be attributed to the operation of natural processes.

Telos. Purpose. Telos is the Greek word meaning end either as final state or goal.

Theism. Belief in a God with aseity who creates the world ex nihilo from the beginning and continues actively to engage the world with ongoing divine activity. Such engagement can take the form of interventionist divine action, such as miracles, or noninterventionist divine action, such as providence or creation continua. Trinitarian Christians tend to be theists.

Theistic Evolution. A family of theological positions that see a convergence between Darwinian evolutionary theory including natural selection with the doctrine of creation.

Theodicy. Literally, the justification of God in the face of a divinely created world that contains evil. In the philosophy of religion, the theodicy problem is the problem of evil formulated in terms of three premises: (1) God is omnipotent or all powerful; (2) God is omnibenevolent or all loving; (3) evil complete with suffering and death are present in the world God has created. This is an intellectual problem because only two of these premises can be affirmed, not all three, without introducing inconsistency.

Theology of Nature. Relying on special revelation, Theology of Nature interprets the natural world in light of understanding God as creator and redeemer. This contrasts with Natural Theology, which relies on general revelation to discern spiritual presence or to prove the existence of God.

Transcendence, Transcendentalism. A theological term designating reality beyond the material and social realm. God or spirit are usually considered transcendent to the physical world, beyond the physical, while being present in the physical.

Two Books. Traditional Christian belief that revelation of God comes courtesy of two media, natural revelation and special revelation. Scientists study the first book and readers of the Bible, the second.

Uniformitarianism. The belief among scientists that the natural processes we witness today also operated in the past and will continue as they are into the future. Uniformitarianism usually opposes episodic jumps or punctuated leaps in evolutionary history; and it certainly opposes saltations or divine interventions.

Variation. Individuals within a population may exhibit slightly different inherited traits. Such differences or variations are acted on by natural selection. Some survive.

Others don't. In the neo-Darwinian model, inherited variations are the result of genetic mutations.

Young Earth Creationism (YEC). Within creationism, the belief that the earth and the entire cosmos as we see it was created less than ten thousand years ago. YEC'ers presume that each of the seven days in Genesis 1:1–2:4a was twenty-four hours long.